# ROOM 1203

## O.J. SIMPSON'S
## LAS VEGAS CONVICTION

## ANDY CALDWELL

WILDBLUE
PRESS

WildBluePress.com

ROOM 1203 published by:
WILDBLUE PRESS
P.O. Box 102440
Denver, Colorado 80250

WILDBLUE PRESS is registered at the U.S. Patent and Trademark Offices.

ISBN 978-1-942290-06-8 Trade Paperback

ISBN 978-1-942290-05-1 eBook

Interior Formatting/Book Cover Design by Elijah Toten www.totencreative.com

# CONTENTS

# INTRO

On a warm Las Vegas evening in September 2007, O.J. Simpson led an assembly of armed henchmen into a hotel room at the Palace Station Hotel and Casino and held two men at gunpoint while they robbed them. Using violence and terror, Simpson stole property under shady circumstances he helped to create and then tried to sell to the world the lie that he was simply taking his own property back. It was an evening of deceit and arrogance that endangered the lives of innocent people and an evening that would result in one of America's most infamous persons being sent to prison.

On the night of Sept. 13, 2007, I was working as a robbery detective for the Las Vegas Metropolitan Police Department with my partner, Det. Eddie LaNeve. With one call, a reported armed robbery in Room 1203 at the Palace Station, my life and career were transformed. The next year of my life was consumed with investigating the events surrounding O.J. Simpson's decision to commit an armed robbery in a Las Vegas hotel and casino.

Former NFL star O.J. Simpson, who was surrounded by figures such as Robert Kardashian during his world-famous double-murder trial and who played the beloved Officer Nordberg from the *Naked Gun* series, had become a man who surrounded himself with thugs who make threats of violence when things don't go their way. His fall from the grace he received from his adoring mainstream fans in the '80s and early '90s was remarkable. But in the sordid underworld of immorality, he was still able to enjoy a life where a different kind of fan would do anything to be around him.

I found myself investigating a crime that at face value was incredibly simple. I also found that the media and much of the public wanted this robbery to be more than it was; people wanted this amazingly dramatic back story that either made his actions more egregious or more innocent. But it was the person of O.J. Simpson and the investment, both positive and negative, that people made in his rise and fall that made a simple investigation become complex and full of unexpected twists and turns.

# CHAPTER I
# CALL TO ROBBERY

Sept. 13, 2007, started out as a slower-than-usual Thursday evening for robberies in Las Vegas. The robbery section for the Las Vegas Metropolitan Police Department was one of the more elite units on the department and detectives usually earned their way in by putting in hard work elsewhere first. The crime of robbery is often misunderstood and the word "robbery" is often used incorrectly to describe burglary. What sets robbery apart is its violent and personal nature. A robbery is when someone uses force or threats of force to take something from you; it's someone walking up to you with a gun pointed at you and saying, "Give me your money!" or someone beating you with a bat before taking your watch. It is a life-changing crime to experience and often creates emotional scars that leave victims feeling unsafe, violated and paranoid and may require intensive therapy to recover from. It is a crime that few people commit and the monsters who do commit it have a violent tendency that leads them to commit it over and over until they are caught. It is a crime that rightly deserves lengthy prison sentences. I was working swing shift as a robbery detective and when it was slow, my partner Eddie and I would leave the office to help uniformed officers handling lower-level robberies that would normally not get a detective to respond to. We heard the dispatcher broadcast a street robbery between two transients who lived in a dry flood control tunnel in the southwest part of Vegas. One of the subjects was reported to be armed with a knife and had taken a wallet from another homeless guy. By the time Eddie and I arrived, the uniformed officers already had the armed suspect in handcuffs and in the back of their black-and-white patrol car.

This type of call would normally take an officer and

partner off the streets for about two hours; but for Eddie and me, we could get it done in about half the time because we specialized in robberies. This would be an easy one for us, but the suspect was a homeless man. Before Eddie was promoted to detective, he worked as a patrol officer in downtown Las Vegas where a majority of the vagrants lived in the late '90s and early 2000s. Eddie earned his spot in the robbery section by working a decoy program in the downtown area. The decoy program ran for only a few years before the plug was pulled on it. I'm still not sure how none of our officers got seriously hurt being decoys. Officers of slight build are ideal candidates to play the decoy, because muggers are more likely to victimize people they can overpower. The decoy officer would volunteer and dress up like a drunken tourist— going as far as even spilling beer on the clothes to smell bad. The officer would wear a wire and have a safe word of "help," and arrest phrase of "What did you do that for?" A team of four to eight officers in plainclothes would stay close, hiding in a van or nearby business so they would come running if they heard the officer call for help over the wire. It was rare the officer called for help, even when surrounded by five or six gangbangers harassing and pushing the officer around. The decoy would have a $20 bill hanging out of a pocket; most of the time, the officer would get pushed and threatened and the suspect would take the money and run. When the decoy said, "What did you do that for?" the rest of the officers would rush the suspect, surround him, and take him down. It was a fun operation for officers to work as long as they were not the decoys. I got to work a few of these with Eddie, but we were never the decoys because both of us are too big to make good victims.

The summer heat of Las Vegas extends into September and the daytime temperatures were still in the 100s; so the body odors are pretty pungent on most of the local transient population. Taking this arrest meant Eddie and I would have to load this suspect in my undercover cloth-seated Nissan

Maxima and drive with him from our office to the jail in downtown Las Vegas behind the Fremont Street Experience. Although the trip to the Clark County Detention Center with a pungent transient would be as unpleasant as you can imagine, it was what we'd have to do before booking the suspect that made Eddie reconsider arresting this particular suspect. As part of the booking process, we would have to remove the suspect's shoes and socks. The smell of removing a vagrant's shoes is pretty bad—especially in the summer heat—but removing the socks is a whole different level of smell that few people will ever experience. Most of the time, the socks are stuck to the skin and, as the socks are peeled off, skin flakes off with them. The material of the sock often feels thicker than it looks from all the sweat and grime build-up. When the sock starts peeling away from the bottom of the heel, the smell hits its worst level; at times, it can be strong be enough to cause a gag reflex. After a couple of minutes pass, the smell becomes manageable and the booking continues like any other arrest.

Even though Eddie wasn't excited to take the arrest, he still agreed it was the right thing to do. The only thing we needed was for one of the uniformed officers to transport the suspect back to our office and we would handle the rest. This was a win-win-win for the officers because they got to catch the bad guy, got the bragging rights of arresting an armed robber, and didn't have to do the paperwork. It was also a win for us as detectives, because we were able to help out the uniformed officers—even though we would have to put up with the smell for a short time.

At about 8:30 p.m., we had only been back at the LVMPD robbery office for a few minutes when my pager went off, alerting me there was a robbery that needed detectives to respond. All of the on-duty robbery detectives receive pager notifications when there is a robbery or kidnapping reported in the City of Las Vegas and the unincorporated areas of Clark County, which had a population of about 1 million people at that time. Each robbery detective was assigned a certain area of town as a specific area of responsibility. It just so happened when my pager went off, it was a reported armed robbery with multiple suspects at the Palace Station Hotel and Casino—in my assigned area. I felt horrible for the uniformed officer in the transient arrest who undoubtedly had his hopes up that he wouldn't have to do the paperwork himself. Had the pager gone off five minutes later than it did, he would have been gone and I would have gotten someone else to cover the Palace Station robbery while Eddie and I did the paperwork. I think he could tell by our hurried footsteps toward him that we had bad news: he would have to finish the paperwork himself.

The information on the pager is limited to the nature of the crime: the location, an event number (which is a recordkeeping number assigned to any event resulting in police action) and basic suspect information. As a police officer, one of the hardest lessons to learn is that most of time, you have to work with limited information that cannot slow how you respond or react when you arrive. So Eddie and I grabbed our duty bags, jumped into my undercover Maxima and headed toward the Palace Station from our office. Within a block, Eddie's phone started to ring; it was our supervisor, Sgt. Rod Hunt. Rod was a great boss. He always had a calm and quiet demeanor about him, but he was a physical fitness junkie so he looked like he could rip anyone's head off with his hands at any given time. He did everything he could to help make our jobs easier; he trusted us to be cops and let us run investigations the best way we knew how, knowing we had the best interests of the victims and our community in our hearts. It was pretty normal for him to call when there was any reported robbery other than street robberies where no one was injured. He usually just wanted to know that we received the pager notification and were responding. But this was not an ordinary call. Eddie laughed for a moment and asked Rod if he was serious.

Eddie is an awesome cop, but at times he is a little rough around the edges. I think his exact words to Rod were, "Are you shitting me?" Eddie listened for a minute or so and told Rod we were headed to the Palace Station and he would give him an update as soon as he knew something. When Eddie got off the phone, he laughed again and, with his New Jersey accent, told me there were multiple victims—and they were reporting one of the robbery suspects was O.J. Simpson.

The moment he told me that O.J. was possibly involved in an armed robbery was one of those moments I can never forget. My instant thoughts were: "How is that even possible? No way could O.J. be that stupid! What if it really is him, the most notorious guy in America?" Eddie and I were not just partners at work; we are also friends outside of work. For a few moments, Eddie and I forgot we were detectives and acted like two buddies who had just heard O.J. Simpson robbed someone. As we pulled into the parking lot of the Palace Station, we both quickly discounted the possibility of O.J. Simpson being involved in a robbery and regained our bearing as robbery detectives.

The Palace Station is only a couple miles from our office, so we arrived within 15 minutes. The parking lot was pretty busy, but I was able to find a spot in the north lot by the main entrance. As we walked into the casino, the chaotic noise of slot machines could be heard in every direction. The seats at the slots and card tables were full for a Thursday evening. There were cocktail waitresses walking around give free drinks to anyone who was gambling. If O.J. Simpson had just committed an armed robbery, it was not going to slow down the activities of the casino floor. We walked to the security kiosk inside the main entrance of the casino, which is elevated so security officers get a better view of everything going on in the casino. I asked if a security officer could take us back to the security office. Las Vegas casinos have their own individual security forces that are larger than most mid-sized town police departments in America; they have dispatchers, advanced surveillance, militaristic command structure and most of the officers are armed. Because of the size of Las Vegas casinos, most police officers need security to show us where the security offices are. One of the security officers, an older gentleman wearing a uniform that from a distance could be mistaken for an LVMPD uniform, asked us to follow him. On the way, I asked him if he had any details about the robbery. He only knew the robbery happened in one of the rooms and the victims were in the main security office. I asked him if he had heard anything about O.J. Simpson being on the property that evening and he said no. Security forces at casinos are good about knowing if there are any high-profile guests on their property. Based on his response, I felt more that Rod's information about O.J. being involved was wrong.

The security guard walked us through the casino floor maze to a door people would never notice unless they were looking for it. In most casinos, the carpet and walls have a way of matching in a monotonous way that causes your eyes to focus on the slot machines and various games. People rarely notice the doors that lead to the working areas that keep all that money flowing and exchanging on the casino floor. He walked us through a large kitchen area with pots and pans clanging and an army of cooks hustling to keep the food flowing and the guests satisfied. Then he led us through an outdoor service area where bread was being delivered, into a hallway on the backside of the main building and to a door with an industrial-style buzzer. The security guard pushed the buzzer and the door was opened from the inside. Eddie and I were greeted by a man in a suit—one of the security supervisors who waved us into the main security office.

There was nothing fancy about this room. It was about 40-foot square with plain white walls and a couple of long folding tables with simple chairs. We walked in to see two large middle-aged men pacing around the room and talking loudly on their phones. One of the initial responding police officers, Officer Lewis, was also in the security office with the victims. The victims had flamboyant personalities and were understandably upset, but they were being so loud that they were distracting me from gaining any details of the robbery from Officer Lewis. I asked them to end their calls and relax so we could get a handle on what was going on, but they weren't calming down quickly enough. Being mindful of the possibility these guys had just been robbed, our attempts to quiet them were at first polite. Eventually, though, it escalated to Eddie demanding they both "sit down and be quiet for a minute." That was the beginning of what would be a rocky relationship between the victims and me.

When the two men, Bruce Fromong and Alfred Beardsley, were able to slow down enough to see Eddie and I were there to help, they began to calm down on their own. Officer Lewis was able to provide me with some preliminary details, but they were limited at this point because when there are multiple witnesses and suspects, it takes time to reconstruct what happened. Fromong and Beardsley had consistently told the LVMPD patrol officers who were first to arrive that O.J. Simpson, along with some other men, had robbed them at gunpoint. Officer Lewis seemed skeptical of Fromong and Beardsley's story and the security supervisor had already told me, "It was never reported that O.J. Simpson had been on the property." After about five minutes, it became clear that I just needed to sit down with one of the victims and have him calmly explain what had happened that evening at the Palace Station. Between the two, Fromong was calmer at this time and a little more coherent. I singled out Fromong to try and get some basic details about what he alleged had happened. About this time, Det. Linda Turner and Rod arrived in the security office to help. Linda and I had gone to the police academy together and she had experience working some big cases, so I was glad to see her and Rod. I gave them what little information I knew and asked them if they could interview Beardsley. After Beardsley went to another room with Linda and Rod, Eddie and I prepared to begin a formal recorded interview with Fromong. Before I got my notepad and recorder situated to start the interview, I was already getting a little frustrated because Fromong was rambling about things such as how he had worked in the California Department of Corrections and so he knows how to handle situations like this. People react differently after they have been the victim of a violent crime, but it is pretty common for men to puff up their chest and act tough even when it is clear they are shaken up inside. This is what Fromong was doing, but because of how loud he and Beardsley were when I first arrived, my empathy was running a little short and I just needed him to stay focused on my questions. Before I start a recorded interview with a victim, I like to explain what I am doing and why I am doing it. Robbery victims can be very scattered in their thoughts and, without some direction, they often tell investigators stories that are all over the map because they will remember a detail they left out and will jump backward to something they already talked about or forward to something that does not make sense yet. I had to bluntly tell him to just stick to answering the questions I ask. He kept mentioning he was "O.J. Simpson's manager" but also that "O.J. robbed" him. It was clear this was going to be a long interview before it even started.

Once I started recording, though, the interview went pretty well. One technique I use to keep victims on track is to ask simple questions and walk them through what had occurred, one question at a time. I was able to get Fromong to stay focused on my questions long enough to find out he lived in North Las Vegas and had come to the Palace Station that night for a pre-arranged viewing and possible sale of his sports memorabilia collection. He was there to meet Beardsley, who was the middleman for the sale to a client named Tom Riccio. Fromong did not know Riccio, but knew Riccio owned a memorabilia business in Los

Angeles. Fromong met Beardsley and Riccio in the hotel lobby, where Riccio them the buyer was going to come to a room Riccio had reserved to view the memorabilia. Riccio led them into Room 1203, followed by a bellman pushing a cart full of Fromong's sports memorabilia. While Fromong was waiting for what he thought was a potential client, O.J. Simpson came in the room with five other men. Two of them had handguns and the group took Fromong's memorabilia collection at gunpoint. Fromong was unwavering in claiming O.J. Simpson was one of the suspects. At this point, I was stuck with two possibilities: I'm either talking to a complete nut job or O.J. Simpson did really rob this guy. I needed to get more details from Fromong, but I also needed to know if this guy was wasting everyone's time. Eddie went up to the surveillance room to ask if he could review the video to see if O.J. Simpson was, in fact, on the property while I continued with the interview.

I took a break from the interview and I walked out to a hallway just outside the security office to have a little privacy. I called Eddie to see if he had found anything. Initially, Eddie was quiet and short with answering me; it was clear he was walking to a spot where he could share information without others hearing. Within a moment, he started to talk a little muffled and said, "You're not going to believe this. It is O.J. Simpson and he did come in with some other dudes and they all left carrying shit they didn't have when they went in." I was a little shocked and I asked him, "Are you sure it's O.J.?" He responded with a little laughter and a little profanity in his New Jersey accent telling me, "There's no mistaking that fucker—it's him!" At that moment, I realized this was going to be huge and I would have to make sure we would not give anyone reason to question our work.

# CHAPTER 2
# VICTIMS AND
# ANOTHER SUSPECT

So now I know something actually happened and it involved O.J. Simpson, but I'm still feeling uncomfortable with Fromong's story. It just didn't make sense. At this point in my career, I had been a robbery detective for four years and I averaged about 20 cases a month assigned to me. After time, you just get to know when something is off. If I remove O.J. Simpson's celebrity from the allegations, then I would not have problems with Fromong's story. But why would O.J. Simpson need to use armed thugs to rob a local memorabilia dealer and why would he do it in a casino where everyone knows they record all public areas? And, as Eddie had said: you can't miss or mistake O.J. Simpson.

By this time in the evening, the LVMPD watch commander had arrived at the Palace Station. The watch commander is the person in charge of all law enforcement operations for any given shift. Watch commanders rarely involve themselves directly in an investigation; they normally monitor what is happening to ensure there are no glaring procedural problems and will request to be briefed when there are lulls in the momentum. They can be a nice resource for investigators because they might not know all the details, but they generally have a good handle on the various activities that are happening. For example, I now have a growing interest in Riccio, and I want to verify he is still at the Palace Station. The watch commander told me that uniformed patrol officers were with Riccio in a hotel room the Palace Station had provided to assist in our investigation.

I went back to interviewing Fromong, but now I'm giving him more credibility. He had calmed down quite a bit from when I first contacted him. As I started the interview again, he explained to me how Beardsley was not really a friend, but more of an acquaintance he knew through the sports memorabilia world. Beardsley had contacted Fromong and asked him if he had O.J. Simpson memorabilia he wanted to sell. Beardsley had claimed there was an auction house in Los Angeles with a buyer who has sought O.J. Simpson memorabilia and was now again looking to buy a large amount of Simpson memorabilia. Beardsley told Fromong the buyer was willing to pay top dollar. Fromong had a large collection and was willing to sell it, so he agreed to meet Beardsley and Riccio, who would bring the unknown buyer to the Palace Station that evening.

Fromong explained how he had worked for O.J. Simpson for more than 15 years and was the director of sales and marketing for a business called Locker 32. The memorabilia market was a means for Simpson to get money under the table, Fromong later explained, so he could avoid paying $33.5 million in civil judgments to the families of his ex-wife, Nicole Brown Simpson, and Ron Goldman. While Simpson was acquitted of the 1994 murders, the victims' families won a wrongful death case against him in 1997. The families had already collected $500,000 from an auction of O.J.'s assets, including his Heisman trophy. If someone paid Simpson $10 or $20 to sign a famous picture of himself, the buyer could then sell the picture for $50 and no one would know of Simpson's involvement. This might not sound like much at first, but a few hundred signatures over the course of a weekend adds up fast.

A few of the memorabilia items Fromong brought to Room 1203 had at one time belonged to Simpson—all of the commemorative plaques and all but one football—but Fromong claimed he had bought them from a man named Mike Gilbert. That was only a small portion of the O.J. Simpson memorabilia Fromong had brought, including hundreds of autographed pictures that Simpson never owned. Fromong figured if this buyer was so big and was willing to pay top dollar, he might also be interested in memorabilia from Joe Montana, Duke Snyder, Pete Rose and West Point. Fromong brought his other memorabilia to show to the potential buyer in hopes the buyer might like those items, too, and Fromong could make maximize his sale.

It was now making more sense why Fromong was at the Palace Station and seems more like a legitimate victim, but his story was painting a shady picture of Beardsley and Riccio.

After he met Beardsley and Riccio in the lobby, they loaded the memorabilia onto a bellman's cart, and followed Riccio to Room 1203, which Riccio had booked before they arrived. The memorabilia was unloaded from the bellman's cart, taken out of the boxes and laid out on the bed (I had not seen the room yet, but it ended up being a room with just one queen bed). The items were laid out so the buyer could get an overall view of the collection. After setting everything out for display, Fromong received a personal call and walked out into the hall just outside of the room to have some privacy. After around 20 minutes, Riccio came out of Room 1203 and said, "They're on their way. Come on in the room." Looking back, Fromong told me, "That hit me a little strange." Fromong went back in the room and continued his phone conversation. Riccio left to go meet the buyer and was gone for a few minutes. The next thing Fromong knew, O.J. and five other men came rushing into the room; the two gunmen already had their guns out and were pointing them at Fromong and Beardsley.

Fromong described how he was standing and was still on the phone when the robbers came in the room. One of the men rushed Fromong and pushed him to the back corner of the room while O.J. Simpson yelled orders at everyone. Both Fromong and Beardsley were cornered and held at gunpoint. As I sat and listened to Fromong describe being pushed around in a small hotel room at gunpoint, I could see his proud shoulders start to fall. Though he was still speaking loudly, his eyes started to glass over and it was clear he was reliving the moment as he recounted it to me. I started to regain some of that empathy I lost when I first met him.

He said O.J. kept yelling, "This is my shit!," barking out that no one was leaving and ordering his men to start bagging up all the property. While his men were stuffing Fromong's property into pillowcases that they took off the pillows from the bed, O.J. kept yelling irrationally, accusing Fromong and Beardsley of stealing and selling his stuff and how he thought they were his friends. Fromong reported one of the men with a handgun said, "We'd handle this shit different in L.A. It wouldn't be this fucking easy." Fromong wasn't sure why the armed man brought up L.A., but it was a statement that scared him the moment it was said.

Fromong said he tried to explain to O.J.—when he could get a word in—that the memorabilia never belonged to Simpson. At one point, Simpson snatched Fromong's phone and, ignoring pleas to return it, said he would leave it at the front desk. O.J. and his armed crew took everything Fromong had laid out on the bed for what he thought was a potential buyer. Fromong, Beardsley and Riccio were left with two baseball bats of Fromong's that were in a corner and all of Riccio's property, including memorabilia for his auction house business.

I don't think Fromong had time up until this point to calmly process everything that happened leading up to the robbery. He had indicated something wasn't right about Riccio's involvement before the interview, but I did not have enough details about the incident to make sense of what he was saying. As he calmly finished telling me what he remembered about the robbery, I could see he was settling more and more on this being a setup and Riccio being behind the robbery. The moment of his slouching posture and watery eyes passed and I could see he was starting to point his anger toward Riccio.

After I finished interviewing Fromong, I met with

Linda and Rod to see what Beardsley's version was. They finished their interview before me and had already talked to Eddie, so they also knew O.J. was involved and there was some truth to what we were being told. Beardsley's story was similar to Fromong's, but he seemed more adamant that Riccio had set them up and orchestrated the robbery. Beardsley reported his sunglasses were stolen during the robbery, but he did not know who took them.

As Linda and Rod gave me a rundown of Beardsley's interview, I picked up on one strange inconsistency. Beardsley said he was contacted by Riccio, who was looking for high-end O.J. Simpson memorabilia for a client. Beardsley had been dealing with Riccio for a couple weeks before this meeting and had faxed a list of items that were going to be up for sale. Fromong never talked about a property list and his involvement seemed like a last-minute afterthought. Beardsley's story of faxing a list to Riccio seemed strange and did not make sense, but the consistent elements of both Fromong's and Beardsley's stories were adding up to armed robbery and kidnapping. The bulk of the property stolen out of the room clearly belonged to Fromong and two of the men who took the property were armed with handguns while Fromong and Beardsley were pushed around and confined in the room.

It was time to go talk with Riccio. One of the security supervisors walked Eddie and me to the room where Riccio was waiting. We entered the hallway from the security office; it was long and zigzagged a couple of times. The hallways in Las Vegas hotels are plush and well kept; everything about them is inviting and comforting. There are no windows or glass doors at the end of the halls, so it is easy let the time of day get away from you. As we rounded the last corner, there was a uniformed police officer sitting in a chair between Room 1203, where the robbery happened, and Room 1204 directly across the hall, where Riccio was being kept. I asked the officer if Riccio had wanted to leave and the officer told me no. I found that to be very odd because in my mind, if he were behind all of this, he would have wanted to leave as soon as possible. In the State of Nevada, police officers are allowed to detain a person only for 60 minutes to further an investigation; if there is no probable cause to arrest after 60 minutes, we are required by law to release the person. Because he never asked to leave, I was not going to concern myself with the 60-minute rule, but if he pushed the issue, I was prepared to arrest him for conspiracy to commit robbery.

Eddie and I took a few moments to plan before going into the room where Riccio was waiting. Conducting quality interviews is one of the most important skills a detective can develop. Victims can sometimes exaggerate what happened and suspects oftentimes minimize their actions, but a good interview can draw out details and inconsistencies to help recreate what actually happened. Interviewing people is one of my strong areas; I can find themes of common ground quickly and create a non-threatening environment relatively fast with victims and suspects. When I interview, it is very important to me that my partner just takes notes and lets me control the interview until I ask them to enter the conversation. This is a courtesy I extend back to any detective or officer conducting an interview. This can be a hard request because my interviews are usually long. It's also important to recognize interviews are fluid and personalities can clash, creating a barrier one detective can't cross but another detective can. I like to start with small talk and see if I can find something other than the crime I'm investigating to talk about such as local sports, summer heat, cars and so forth. Interview skills are put to their greatest test in interviewing suspects. When investigating robberies, I could use a common talking point—such as providing for the care of kids—to offer a justification as to why someone might commit a robbery. I might talk about the importance of providing for family to keep them safe and how I can understand how someone would be willing to take extreme measures to do that. I can use themes like that to suggest a mitigating circumstance they will think makes their crime look noble and, after taking time in building a good relationship, I have a pretty good success rate at extracting confessions.

At this point, I believe Riccio is involved, but I want to talk with him to learn as much as possible about what had happened. Our initial plan was to go into the room and I would start the interview to see where it went. I knocked at the door and a man I assumed was Riccio answered. He had an odd, almost fake, East Coast accent, but he appeared happy to see us and invited us in. The interview seemed to be off to a good start. Within a few moments, it became clear he was one of those people who thinks the louder and faster he talks, the more people will believe him. He had no interest in telling me what actually happened or answering questions. He just wanted to tell the version of the story he came up with that minimized his involvement in the robbery. He admitted to setting up the meeting, but he claimed he thought the property that was being brought to the room had been stolen from O.J. and that O.J. was going to come and get what belonged to him. He told me multiple times he had no idea Simpson and his friends were going to bring guns. Riccio was not yelling, but his loud voice filled the small hotel room and he flailed his arms around as if he were passionately pleading with me to believe what he was saying. The problem with his story was he knew what was in Room 1203 before he went to get Simpson and the others armed suspects. Then he led them back to the room and had to have unlocked the door to let them in to commit the crime. The truth was clearly subjective to whatever Riccio needed it to be at the moment to avoid being held accountable for a crime in which he was clearly involved. Regardless of what I asked, he kept loudly and rapidly saying what he wanted to say. This guy was like a wind-up doll that would not stop. All my experience with interviewing suspects has taught me that if they are going to talk, let them talk and record it. My experience and knowledge went out the window and within five minutes of being in the room, he pissed me off so bad that I put him in cuffs and read him his Miranda rights. All that mattered to me at that point were the simple facts he had admitted: being in contact with Simpson before the robbery and being involved in setting up. I was done with Riccio and I didn't want to have any more of my time wasted listening to his self-serving nonsense.

I needed to search Room 1203 and allow the LVMPD criminalistics section (CSI) to collect evidence. Since the room was rented to Riccio, he could claim an expectation of privacy, preventing police from searching and processing the room without his consent or a search warrant. Riccio also had a vehicle in the parking lot, which I wanted to have searched for evidence of his involvement in the robbery.

In 2007, I had two options for obtaining a search warrant under these circumstances. I could go back to the office and type up an affidavit detailing the location to be searched, the items I am looking for and the justification for the search. I could then contact an on-call deputy district attorney to get an approval, drive to a judge's home, wake the judge up at about midnight and finally get the search warrant signed. The other option was a telephonic search warrant. Rather than typing anything up, I would just call the on-duty deputy district attorney and give the details to get an approval. The next call is to a judge on a recorded line on which I simply dictate the same details that would be in a typed search warrant while the judge listens and the recording gets typed up later. The recording and a verbal authorization to sign the judge's name to a telephonic search warrant was faster and accomplished the same thing as a typed-out search warrant.

I opted for the telephonic search warrant. I called the on-call deputy district attorney and a lady answered the phone. I didn't recognize her name, but I had the right number and she was clearly the on-call deputy. After I finished giving her the details of the robbery and of O.J. Simpson's involvement, there was a moment of silence on the line. I was a little taken back that she had to think about the details; I had written and called in more search warrants that I can remember and I had a good grasp on what acceptable probable cause was. I asked her if I had her approval and she responded by telling me, "I'm new and I can't approve a search warrant involving O.J. Simpson." She asked me for my phone number and told me she would call back. Within a few minutes, my phone rang; it was Chief Deputy District Attorney Frank Coumou. I knew Frank and had worked a few cases with him. He chuckled a bit and asked me what I had. I ran the details by him and he didn't even hesitate in giving his approval to proceed with the search warrant. While I had him on the phone, I asked his opinion on arresting Riccio. Prosecutors are funny about probable cause arrests. They are quick to point out it is up to the police whether to arrest without a warrant, but then they state their opinion. Frank offered up a valuable thought that I did not want to hear because I was mad at Riccio; he suggested that Riccio sounded like he might be a valuable witness in the near future and if it turned out he could not help with the investigation, I could arrest him later. For as much as I understood what Frank was saying and agreed on a practical level, I wasn't going into the room to take the cuffs off Riccio. So after discussing what Frank had suggested with Eddie, I asked him to go to Riccio, uncuff him and explain that he was free to go for now, but his vehicle and property in Room 1203 would not be released until we were finished with our investigation at the Palace Station. Riccio stayed in the room across the hall and waited.

I called Judge Ann Zimmerman, who was one of the judges on a list the DA's office provided for telephonic search warrants. I read off the details and she approved the search warrant without question. Once the search warrant was approved, the CSIs went into the room to process it for evidence of a crime. Eddie and I went into the room to look around, as did other detectives and supervisors from the robbery section. As criminalistics were processing the room, Lt. Clint Nichols, the robbery section lieutenant, came walking up to me and told me that LVMPD command staff had decided that O.J. Simpson would not be arrested that night.

In that moment, I knew it could be argued that if what happened was bad enough to send O.J. to prison, why did we not arrest him the moment we knew he was involved? It opened the door to for a conspiracy theory of police making something out of nothing just to nail O.J. It was rare for administrators to directly involve themselves in an investigation and even rarer to make a decision about an investigation without involving the lead detective. As a detective, I recognized I might completely disagree with a decision from command staff, but I have a chain of command and unless what they order me to do is unlawful, I have to follow orders. Lt. Nichols knew I would not be happy about being told I could not arrest an armed robbery suspect, so he had already arranged to have a team of detectives maintain surveillance on Simpson until the decision not to arrest could be revisited. I didn't like it, but it was not a decision worth fighting with all the other things I had going on at the moment.

It was never my intention to use the search warrant for Room 1203 in a traditional way of looking for drugs or guns. It was my intent to obtain a search warrant to provide a legal means to recover forensic evidence including fingerprints or residual DNA to help identify the unknown suspects involved in the armed robbery and provide evidence of Simpson being in the room. The search warrant did allow for me to conduct a traditional search, but I did not see the need. My decision to not conduct a full search of the room would end up being a pretty big mistake for which I am solely responsible.

The search of Riccio's car did not yield any further

evidence and after the room was done being processed, Eddie and I gave access to it back to Riccio. It was undeniable that Riccio and I were not going to have a good relationship after our initial meeting. Riccio seemed to respond better to Eddie, who instructed him to contact us with any new or forgotten details. He also told Riccio we would be back in touch as the investigation progressed.

By the time we were wrapping up our investigation at the Palace Station, it was daybreak on Sept. 14. As we were leaving the Palace Station property, the news media was starting to set up in parking lots to the north and the south of the casino. After already being at work for about 18 hours, Lt. Nichols told our squad of detectives that the robbery/ homicide bureau commander wanted a full briefing back at the robbery office.

# CHAPTER 3
# TO CHARGE OR NOT TO CHARGE

As Eddie and I walked out of the Palace Station, we were surrounded by the regular casino goers of Las Vegas who had no idea a crime committed there that would dominate the news cycle for the next couple of weeks and result in America's most infamous man going to prison. Even at 7 a.m., the chairs in front of the slot machines were full and people cheering at the craps tables could be heard throughout the casino floor. There are regulars from an older generation who come in the morning hours to beat the extreme heat and crowds. Mixed in with them are the all-night partiers who have no idea they have gambled the entire night away.

It had been a long shift and our exhaustion was exacerbated by walking out into the morning heat of Las Vegas. Eddie and I flopped into my unmarked Maxima and I drove back to the robbery office. It was a quiet drive—not because we didn't have things to talk about, but because we were tired and knew we still had a good amount of work to do before we could go home. When I was pulling into our office parking lot, my phone rang. It was Rod. "Are you close?" he asked. He was in a hurry; no one from our squad had made it back to the office yet. "Tell the guys the captain is waiting," he told me. "Just come straight up to the conference room."

The Las Vegas Metropolitan Police Department functions like a county sheriff's department. The head of our agency is the elected sheriff of Clark County; at the time of Simpson's armed robbery, it was Sheriff Doug Gillespie. He had an under sheriff, two assistant sheriffs, six deputy chiefs and 16 captains with almost 4,000 employees. The captains are the bureau commanders, and are usually the highest-ranking officer that detectives will interact with. That interaction is limited to the occasional passing in the hallways or the sporadic question about a high-profile case that you might be working about which they might need details for a briefing or media release. Captains are oftentimes the ones who make unpopular administrative decisions dealing with things such as staffing levels, schedules, when overtime could be worked and employee discipline issues. In functioning like a military chain of command, detectives have two buffers between the captain and us: our sergeant and lieutenant. A briefing from the detectives called by our captain is more stressful for our sergeant than it is for us. If the captain is pissed about something, it won't be directed at us. We would leave the room and he would go off on our sergeant and lieutenant. We had a great captain at the time, so it wasn't likely that he would get mad at much. But it was clear Rod was not happy with how long it took the rest of the squad and me to get to the captain's conference room.

The robbery/homicide bureau is on the third floor of the building where all the detectives worked. By 7:30 a.m., the day shift detectives were all starting to fill the building. Rumors were clearly starting to circulate around the department about the robbery section possibly arresting O.J. Simpson. As a result, I kept getting calls from old friends in the department who wanted to know what was going on. After turning my phone off, I made it in the conference room with Eddie before Rod and Lt. Nichols. Capt. Jim Dillon was joking with Det. Jason Leavitt and Det. Erik Wilds. Even though Capt. Dillon was part of the department's command staff, he was a cop's cop. He didn't come off as thinking he was better than we are; he just had a different job with different responsibilities. That made him easier than most captains to talk with and it made me want to do the best job I could for him. After a couple of sarcastic comments about making him wait, he was ready to get started without Rod and Lt. Nichols, even though they were in the building.

It was during this meeting that it became clear to me

there was an elephant in the room, but no one was going to talk about it: if O.J. Simpson got away with two murders—and was arrogant enough to come to our town and commit a violent crime—then he deserved to get nailed and nailed hard.

But there was also an unspoken fear that if things fell apart, it could come back to make our department look bad.

I started the briefing chronologically, covering step by step what I knew up to that point. As I was briefing the captain, there was some disagreement about whether we thought a robbery charge would stick. To my surprise, Eddie chimed in and said he didn't think we had enough yet to risk making an arrest. He and I had not talked about it yet; that was the first time I heard Eddie voice questions. The captain wanted to know what Eddie's reservations were and he unloaded about his feelings about the untrustworthiness of Beardsley, Fromong and Riccio. Eddie believed they were all full of crap. He was uncomfortable with how they all knew each other and how Fromong at one time worked for Simpson. Eddie's concerns were valid and worth discussing because this case was going to get national attention.

By this point in our briefing, Rod had made it into the conference room. We were all a little tired and a little short with each other, but this was an important issue that needed to be hammered out because there is no path for moving forward if the lead detective and his partner disagree about a robbery charge being able to stick. In police investigations, there is a truth that is not often embraced by supervisors: the detectives who actually conduct the investigations on a regular basis have a better grasp on the practical application of the law and on what can move forward and what can't. Fortunately, both Capt. Dillon and Rod were the type of supervisors who trusted us to work through investigative issues without micromanaging us. There were five detectives in the room: Det. Leavitt, Det. Wilds, Linda, Eddie and me. We started walking through the elements of the crime as if the captain were not sitting there. If it were any other case, the captain probably would have left and told us to let him know when we figured out the direction we were going. But for this one, he stayed and intently listened.

At this point, I didn't know all the details of what led up the robbery, but I had a pretty good handle on what happened in Room 1203 at the Palace Station. As the five of us discussed the incident, we went back to the basics of looking at the Nevada Revised Statute for the elements of robbery. There are four basic elements that must be met. The first element to consider is whether personal property was unlawfully taken. No matter how we looked at it, the suspects took property that belonged to Fromong and Beardsley. The next element of robbery is that the personal property had to be taken from the person or in his presence. This was another easy one: the suspects not only took the Simpson, Montana, Rose and West Point memorabilia that belonged to Fromong in his presence, Simpson also took Fromong's cell phone out of his hand. The same is true for Beardsley; his sunglasses were taken in his presence. Next, we have to consider if the taking of the property was against the will of Fromong and Beardsley, which was also another easy one. The last element to consider meeting to make the crime a robbery is if the property was taken by means of force or violence or fear of injury. Both victims reported that force was used and the presence of the handguns make this element a given. Even though it was reported that only two of the men had handguns, everyone involved is viewed as having committed the same crime. After going through the elements, there was universal agreement that O.J. Simpson had committed the crime of robbery with a deadly weapon.

There are a couple of crimes that I can automatically attach once I determine I am moving forward with the robbery charge. If there is more than one suspect, then there is a conspiracy. Also, because the crime is a felony that happened inside a building and handguns were used, it is also a burglary with a firearm. Burglary is a charge most people outside of law enforcement confuse with other crimes. Burglary is a crime of intent. In Nevada, if you enter into any structure with the intent to commit a felony, then you have committed burglary. If a person commits a felony after entering a structure, I don't need to prove intent, because intent is established by the fact the felony occurred. So as we sat in the conference room kicking around elements of the crimes and the known details, Eddie and I ended up in agreement that it was absolutely a robbery, we could prove it and we should move forward.

In our criminal justice system, there is an assumption of innocence until proven guilty; that does not apply to me as the investigator. When I arrest someone, I am submitting to the courts that I believe the suspect *is* guilty, not that the suspect *might* be guilty. I never want to arrest someone who I do not completely believe is guilty of the crime. Under the circumstances, I think Capt. Dillon and Rod appreciated the care we exercised in considering the details and the elements of the crimes. I can look back and say it was right for Eddie to express his concerns about the character of the victims and to question if we should move forward.

Capt. Dillon now exercised his administrative authority over us. There are two ways at this point to move forward with arresting O.J. Simpson. The simplest way would have been a probable cause arrest. In simple terms, that means when I learned facts and circumstances that would cause a reasonable person to believe a crime (robbery) had been committed, I would exercise my commission to enforce the laws of the State of Nevada and arrest Simpson and book him into the Clark County Detention Center, where he would be brought before a judge to ensure his civil rights were not violated. If it were up to me, at that point, I would have said, "Let's go arrest him." I was confident in what I had. It is important to note that the police have arresting authority, but prosecuting the crime in Nevada is up to the District Attorney's Office. The only downside to making a probable cause arrest of a figure like O.J. Simpson is if the DA's office decided not to move forward because prosecutors felt they could not prove the case. Then I would have egg on my face and, by default, the LVMPD would get a black eye. The other way to proceed was for me to submit a request to the DA's Office for an arrest warrant. In requesting an arrest warrant, I present a written affidavit that contains the circumstances known to me through the investigation. I would request prosecutors approve the charges and have a judge sign the warrant in agreement that there is sufficient evidence to arrest and move forward with a prosecution. The only downside to pursuing an arrest warrant is the suspect gets to walk free until the warrant is approved. Capt. Dillon directed me to pursue the arrest warrant.

Capt. Dillon also expressed operational security concerns for our investigation. Normally, when a detective completes paperwork, a copy is kept in a working case file and the original is submitted to the LVMPD records section to be stored for future access. In the 1996 Tupac Shakur murder investigation, an unknown employee accessed photos and, without authorization, released information to the media. Transparency is a good thing, but it can unnecessarily slow the process of an investigation. If someone leaks information about suspects police are looking to talk with or items police are looking for, then suspects can hide and items can be destroyed. It is easier to have an element of surprise while conducting an investigation. Capt. Dillon directed our robbery squad to not send copies of paperwork related to our investigation to the records section, to keep all photographic evidence locked in Lt. Nichols' office and to keep the working case file locked in Rod's office. He then gave me the order I knew was coming; "I want the request for the arrest warrant submitted this morning to the district attorney himself and I want you to wait for his response."

Nevada has a different political make-up than most states.

The majority of the industry and population is centered in Clark County, so the elected Clark County officials are generally viewed as having more political clout than those from any other county and more influence than some of the elected state officials. So Capt. Dillon just ordered me to prepare a request for an arrest warrant, and rather than submitting it through normal channels, to take it to the head guy and then tell the district attorney that I was going to wait for his response. I already knew that was not going to go over too well, but I also knew I was going to have to do it.

The entire squad agreed to stay and help me get the request for the arrest warrant completed. Eddie typed details about what he saw on the video surveillance at the Palace Station. Linda typed details of her interview with Beardsley. Erik and Jason started working on compiling all the paperwork for the packet. Linda and Eddie emailed me what they had typed and I added their details to my affidavit requesting the arrest warrant for robbery with a deadly weapon, conspiracy to commit robbery, burglary with a firearm and conspiracy to commit burglary for Orenthal James Simpson. As I signed my affidavit, I did a quick review of the packet to make sure everything was in order. It was about 10 a.m. on the morning of the 14th, and by this time day, the office was full of detectives and support personnel going about their daily routines. Rod was in his office and was clearly beat from the long shift. I told him the packet was done and we were going to be heading down to the DA's Office. Rod wanted me to keep him updated with any change. Eddie and I grabbed our bags and headed toward the hallway, which led to the elevator. For the most part, the people in the office had kept their distance from Eddie and me once we had started working on the arrest warrant. As we walked out of the office, we were met with multiple detectives telling us "good luck." I could not get the thought out of my mind that I held in my hands a set of documents that could result in the arrest of O.J. Simpson.

We rode the elevator down to the first floor and walked out to my department vehicle. Eddie sat down in the passenger seat and asked, "Do you think the DA will approve it?" I laughed and said, "It's O.J. Simpson. I don't know." The paperwork was done and from here, it looked like all Eddie and I had left to do was to play a waiting game. On our way down, Eddie asked me if I knew District Attorney David Roger very well. I didn't. I had worked a few cases with him, but my interaction with him was limited and my opinion of him at that time was that he was cold and unapproachable.

The District Attorney's Office is located in the Clark County Regional Justice Center in downtown Las Vegas. The Regional Justice Center also houses the courts, so if the DA approves the warrant, it could then be walked over to one of the courtrooms to be signed by a judge and then O.J. could be arrested.

Parking is always a nightmare at the Regional Justice Center. The loading and unloading areas are constantly packed with marked police vehicles because when on-duty police officers are subpoenaed to court, they need to able to get to the vehicle relatively fast to be able to respond to an emergency. The good short-term parking is often clogged with couples applying for their marriage licenses. Eddie and I had to park two blocks away on the side where the Marriage License Bureau is. As we walked to the building, there were street solicitors standing outside the Marriage License Bureau trying to drum up business for the various wedding chapels in the downtown area. As couples walked by, the solicitors hand them information brochures about the different types of services their business offers; it is one of the strangest forms of commercialism I can imagine. We walked up the steps to enter the building through a special entrance for employees of the courts that police officers use. The Regional Justice Center, like any other courthouse, is a fascinating clash of cultures—standing in one elevator, you can have police officers, hard-core gang members, victims and their families, violent criminals out on bail, lawyers, expert witnesses, reporters and the occasional retiree who likes to watch court proceedings. Once we were in the building, we walked through the large atrium area where a couple hundred people were seeking out the various services offered at the court. This day was like any other; there was a long line of people paying their traffic tickets, crying families upset with how things happened in the courts clumping around seating areas and groups of lawyers standing around telling each other how great they are. The Regional Justice Center has 17 floors and only a few elevators; most the time, they are packed and make frequent stops. There is escalator access for the first three floors and, luckily for us, the DA's Office is on the third floor. Eddie and I made our way to the escalators and rode up to the third floor. As I stepped off the escalator and started toward the DA's Office, I saw Roger round a corner, walking toward the escalators.

I would imagine being the district attorney in a large jurisdiction has perks, but I also imagine it has its drawbacks, too. As Roger walked toward the escalator, a couple guys in suits were talking with him and he only made it a few steps until someone interrupted his discussion by offering a passing greeting. I was not there for social reasons and I didn't want to be lumped in with the various people who are trying to be noticed by the district attorney; I legitimately need to talk with him and knew I was going to have to interrupt his conversation. In general, detectives in the robbery section wear casual business attire and adhere to a clean grooming standard. I was approaching the district attorney in the same clothes I'd worn for almost 24 hours straight and my 5 o'clock shadow was well past 5 o'clock. "Mr. Roger, can I have a moment, please?"

As I got close enough to shake his hand, I introduced myself. I don't think he remembered my name, but he clearly recognized me from cases I worked in the past. It was clear he knew the request for arrest warrant was coming sometime that morning, but he just didn't know when or from whom. The guys in suits walking with him stopped, too, and right there by the escalator on the third floor of the Regional Justice Center, I handed District Attorney Roger the packet requesting an arrest warrant for O.J. Simpson. I am 6-feet, 5-inches with an outgoing personality. I don't know anyone who would describe Roger as a tall man and I think it is fair to describe his personality as reserved. Roger has a unique way of making eye contact even with our remarkable height difference. His head always has a slight tilt down and he looks up above his glasses as he talks with people. It makes him very difficult to read. When I handed the packet to Roger, he put on his glasses, looked at it and said, "Okay." That was it: "Okay." I stood there for a moment and told him I was instructed to wait for a decision. He took pause and politely told me that he would review my request and let me know. For as polite as his delivery was, the message was received loud and clear—how dare I try to place the proverbial monkey on his back of arresting O.J. Simpson then try to make him rush his decision? In this short encounter, I was reminded that the police do not dictate who gets prosecuted and for as much as I wanted an approval on the spot, I also found comfort in the check and balance of the system to make every effort to protect people from wrongful prosecution. Before I left, Roger gave me his business card with his cell phone number and told me to notify him directly if I make any arrests.

With those instructions, Eddie and I walked back to the down escalators and headed for the exit. Capt. Dillon had asked me to call him with the DA's answer, but there was no way I wanted to deliver that message. Instead, I called Rod to advise him that the DA had basically said he would let me know when he was good and ready and not a moment sooner. I think Rod knew that response was coming because he didn't seem too concerned. Rod told us that we needed to get back to the office because O.J. had called and he wanted to talk with us.

# CHAPTER 4
## O.J. TALKS

At that time, I lived in a small farming community about an hour northeast of Las Vegas and I was having growing concerns about my drive home after this shift. I was well past the 24-hour mark and I knew if O.J. did want to talk with me, I would need some prep time and something to eat. Eddie and I stopped at an In-N-Out Burger on the way back to the office. As we waited in the drive-thru, we started talking about how we were going to identify the other suspects involved. Eddie flipped through the pictures he was able to get printed from the surveillance video at the Palace Station and held up a photo of all the suspects in the hotel lobby before the robbery. I couldn't help but laugh. In the picture was a guy who was on top of the world 15 years ago. A football hero, a movie star, a TV personality. He was a household name. And now, he was hanging out with what looked like two wannabe gangsters and three out-of-place over-the-hill guys. If I weren't looking at a picture, I would not have believed it. We paid for our food and ate it on the way back to the office. By the time we arrived, I was no closer to having an idea of how to identify the other suspects than when we first started talking about it.

As my food started to settle and I started to feel like a human again, Eddie and I started brainstorming some ideas while walking back into our office building. We knew O.J. was staying at the Palms Resort and Casino and that he lived in Florida, so it was not likely he drove to Las Vegas. These are rough starting points, but they are starting points. We could locate and get the records from the flight O.J. probably came to Vegas on to see if there was anyone else on the flight who was with him. We also could check with the Palms to see if he checked in with anyone. At this point, we didn't have much else to work with, but in my experience, when you start shaking things up, new leads surface and eventually, you find what you are looking for.

We walked into the robbery office, which was a big, open bay with approximately 45 cubicles; the four corners of the bay had individual private offices for the robbery sergeants. As we walked in, Eddie and I sat our bags down at our desks and headed to Rod's office. Rod had attempted to contact Simpson by phone at the number Riccio had given us the night before. There was no answer, so Rod left a message asking Simpson to call him back. Simpson called back, but Rod missed the call and Simpson left a message. After the back and forth of phone tag, Rod was able to get through to Simpson and tell him we would like to get his side of the story about what happened at the Palace Station. O.J. told Rod, "I'll have my attorney meet me at my room in the Palms and we will sit down and talk with you." Simpson agreed to talk with us at 12:30 p.m.

A detective's ability to conduct a good interview is one of the key areas that sets a great detective apart from an average detective. The ability to apply the laws governing police investigations appropriately and still create an environment in which people want to tell their story is instrumental to an investigation. The biggest hurdle when talking with a suspect is Miranda rights. This is a rule that sounds good in the sterile setting of a courtroom and the safety of a classroom, but it is an offense to victims of crime and the people tasked with the responsibility to protect the innocent. Imagine walking through a park at 10 p.m. and being confronted by a man wearing a black ski mask and black gloves, armed with a handgun. As he points the gun at you, he demands money and because it takes you more than a second to respond, he beats you with the butt of the pistol and takes your wallet or purse as you lay beaten and bleeding alone in the park while the suspect runs away. Someone calls 9-1-1 for you and the police respond to the area looking for a suspect matching the very basic description you were able to provide in the few seconds you had before you were violently pistol-whipped. The police look in the direction you saw the suspect run away. In a construction site, an officer looks in a portable toilet. The officer sees the butt of a handgun sticking out in the toilet hole, above the mix of used toilet paper, human waste and blue liquid. Looking closer, the officer also sees black gloves, a black ski mask and a wallet or purse matching the description of what the suspect took from you. After fishing out the items, it is clear all the forensic evidence has been destroyed and your cash is the only thing gone. Officers stop a 20-year-old white male of about the same height and build as the suspect who robbed you. He has prior arrests for possession of illegal narcotics, battery and carrying a concealed weapon, but when you are brought to see him, all you can say is he is about the same size. The man who has been stopped changed his story a couple of times about where he was coming from and where he was going. When he consented to a search of his pockets, there were five crumpled up $20 bills; you had four $20 bills in your wallet. The man is engaging in small talk with the officers when a detective arrives. Here is where Miranda rights make me want to pull my hair out. As a detective, I would recognize my only hope for an arrest under these circumstances is a confession from a young man who has a criminal history and probably knows he would go to prison if he were caught for an armed robbery. I introduce myself and establish a relationship, but before I ask about the robbery, I have to tell this guy, "You have the right to remain silent. Anything you say can be used against you in a court of law. You have the right to consult with an attorney before questioning. You have the right to the presence of an attorney during questioning. If you cannot afford an attorney, one will be appointed before questioning. Do you understand these rights?" So, basically, the bad guy who is sharp enough to destroy the evidence of his crime is now told by the police, "You don't need to cooperate and if you do, I am going to use anything you say to put you in prison." After giving multiple accounts as to his actions during and after the time of the robbery, he now invokes his rights and stops talking. With no evidence or positive identification, the probable suspect walks away and not much else can be done. Miranda rights are a hard pill to swallow in circumstances like this and although this scenario might sound extreme, it is all too often detectives that need confessions and suspects hide behind the rules of the system that protect them more than the victims they hurt.

The application of Miranda rights has a two-prong requirement. A person must be in custody or be in a position or place where a reasonable person would think they are not free to leave or free to ask the police to leave. So if a person were stopped while driving a car by an officer using emergency lights, that person is not free to leave. If a person is placed in handcuffs, that person is not free to leave. The perception of being in custody can get muddied up pretty easy and one of the ways it can get a little muddy is when a person is surrounded by multiple officers. Though the officers might not be detaining the person, the person can potentially feel forced to cooperate and not free to leave due to feeling surrounded or overwhelmed. The second prong involves asking questions about a crime. Both prongs are required to necessitate a Miranda warning. If a person is in custody or can claim a feeling of not being free to leave, that person can still make incriminating statements without having Miranda rights read by an officer.

In considering the scenario where the victim was robbed and pistol-whipped in the park, then a possible suspect was stopped but there was no further evidence to go on, you can see how important understanding the application of Miranda rights can be. There is no Miranda requirement if a detective walks up to a suspect who was handcuffed and not yet free to leave, introduces himself and says, "What's going on?" Both prongs of the Miranda requirement are not met; the subject is in custody, but the detective has not asked about the crime. Now, if the suspect responds to that general question with a confession or explanation of why he robbed the victim, everything he said is usable. But if the detective has not advised the subject of his Miranda rights and asked a question such as, "Why did you rob that guy?," then gets a confession or explanation, that is not usable.

As we sat down to consider our upcoming interview with Simpson, there was a consideration of Miranda and how it applied. O.J. already had told Rod he has an attorney and the attorney would be present; if that were true, then we would not have to worry about Miranda because most attorneys won't let their clients talk to police. I was not convinced O.J.'s attorney would be there, so we still needed a plan. A few things I had to consider were that O.J. invited us to him and as long as it was only two or three non-uniformed detectives, it would be hard for him to say he was in custody or not free to ask us to leave his room at the Palms. If his attorney was not present and he was willing to talk, there would be no need to advise him of his Miranda rights.

I was going to conduct the interview and normally, there would be no question that Eddie would accompany me on an interview. As I've mentioned before, Eddie can have a short temper and we were all running short on sleep. We decided it would be best if Linda went with us on the interview. Also, under normal circumstances, it would be just two of us in the interview and I can't remember ever having a supervisor participate in an interview. However, this was O.J. Simpson, one of the most recognizable figures in pop culture and undoubtedly everything I did or did not do was going to be heavily scrutinized, so Rod wanted to go, too. Rod accompanying us was a reminder of the importance of being flexible. One danger I always try to avoid is being inflexible so even though we had a general plan in place, if it were clear that Linda or Rod had a better connection with Simpson, then I would gladly transition out of the primary role and just take notes.

As we got ready to leave our office, Rod informed the surveillance squad watching Simpson that we were on our way and would be contacting Simpson in his room. We left our office in separate vehicles, in hopes that after the interview was over, we would be able to go home and get some rest. The Palms Resort and Casino, like the Palace Station, is not on the Las Vegas Strip. It was a newer resort and had a different feel about it than most other off-Strip resorts; it was and is well known as a party resort. It was farther away from our office than the Palace Station and took about 20 minutes to drive to in mid-day traffic. We all parked on the north side and met out in front by the main lobby entrance. Even on a Friday afternoon at the Palms, there was a steady flow of limousines at its main entrance. The Palms attracts a younger crowd, so it's not just the traditional limousines that come and go, it is also a mix of the larger Excursion and Humvee limos full of young adults who come to Vegas to embrace as much of the party atmosphere as they can for the time they are here. There was a doorman dressed in a black suit greeting and sending off the guests as they came and went.

As we walked into the main entrance, we were hit with a blast of refreshing cool air and met with the traditional sounds of a Las Vegas casino. The music is a little louder and a blend of what is popular with the party crowd—yet the design of what you see when you walk in is classy and looks expensive. The dealers and cocktail waitresses seem to be from a younger generation and are more engaged with the guests. The cheers from guests doing well at the craps tables are a little louder and seem to generate more excitement on the casino floor. It feels like the Palms designed an environment to draw in and entertain a younger crowd with a taste for the finer things in life.

It was not lost on me that O.J. Simpson was staying at what was well known as the party resort in Las Vegas. I couldn't help but to think back to the surveillance picture Eddie held up earlier of the former superstar with his wannabe gangster and midlife crisis friends and how predictable it was that someone clinging to his glory days would want to be at the Palms. In my experience, the Palms regularly sees some of the most famous present-day stars, but the classier older generation often frequents places such as the Wynn, Caesars Palace and MGM. Not Simpson. He was the old guy still wanting to live with the party crowd.

I walked to the registration desk to confirm Simpson's room number and find out if there were other people registered to the room. O.J. was staying in a suite, which meant we would need special access to get to his floor. Eddie and I joined Rod and Linda, who were speaking with one of the security guards at the Palms wearing a formal uniform that resembled a black suit. Eddie would go up to O.J.'s floor with us and wait out in the hallway while I conducted the interview. We asked the security guard to escort us up to O.J.'s floor. There wasn't much conversation as we waited for the elevator. There is a good camaraderie between police officers and casino security, but it is not the same brotherhood where we feel like we can let our guard down when it is just us. When we got into the elevator, the security guard had to swipe an access card, and then push the button for the floor we wanted to reach. The ride up was relatively quiet and when we reached the floor, the security guard pointed us in the right direction and waited by the elevator.

One of the guys from the surveillance squad was sitting in a chair by the elevator and we all greeted each other. Here is another notable difference that surrounded this investigation; customarily, officers and detectives are not to acknowledge surveillance detectives in public. As robbery detectives, we generally dressed casually and did not take excessive measures to conceal our badges or firearms. If someone were watching for the police, they would have easily identified Eddie and me as detectives by us being greeted by the surveillance detective; his cover was blown. When the target of surveillance is at home, or in this case in his room, it requires minimal personnel to maintain adequate coverage. At this time, there were six surveillance detectives assigned to monitor Simpson and we just met one by the elevator.

The detectives assigned to work surveillance on the LVMPD are proficient at their jobs. If I did not know them from the past, I would not be able to pick them out in a crowd. They are skilled at fitting into their environment and blending into the background where even if you were looking for them, you would likely miss them.

As we turned down the hall toward O.J.'s suite, three more surveillance detectives stood behind a pillar, visiting with each other while waiting for the two surveillance detectives who were closer to the room to signal that the target was moving. They were working with the Palms security and had a room in the same hall as Simpson's, so the hall could be monitored without a detective just waiting for Simpson to come out of his room.

As Rod, Linda and I approached Simpson's suite, Eddie stayed back in the hall. Rod knocked on the door, and within a few moments, the door swung open and there was O.J. Simpson. This was and is a moment that is hard to reconcile in my mind. As I stood there—a detective tasked with investigating a crime and thinking I was going to conduct this interview just like any other—I was a little star struck. O.J. is not a big, imposing figure. In fact, he was smaller than I would have ever imagined a former NFL player to be. His charismatic personality came shining through the moment he opened the door. With a great big smile and animated arm movements, he invited us into his suite. Here is where that flexibility in interviews became paramount; he leaned out into the hallway and waved Eddie in also. But that wasn't all. The surveillance detectives who take pride in their ability to work undetected—Simpson had spotted them, too, and waved them into the room. As everyone piled into the suite, I had to laugh to myself as I thought I would probably come in, too, if I were in their position. As he waved everyone in, Simpson told me his lawyer was not there yet, but he should be there shortly, so we could wait inside for him.

As I walked past Simpson, I had a moment of realization that helped me to get over my feeling of being star struck. O.J. was wearing the same clothes as he was in the surveillance video from the robbery the night before: a light blue, disheveled polo shirt and blue jeans. I was only vaguely familiar with the 1994 murder case in Los Angeles that O.J. Simpson was tried for. Though I did not know the details of the murders, investigation or trial, I was not blind to the cultural references and jokes about O.J. Simpson getting away with murder. I grew up just north of Los Angeles, but during the murder and trial, I was in the Army station in Georgia and it seemed like it was a world away. It was a busy time in my life as a soldier and husband with a young baby, and I only caught bits and pieces on the news of what was going on. I did remember seeing pictures of the victims Nicole Brown and Ron Goldman. Linda, Rod and I were the first ones in Simpson's suite and had a moment to survey the room while O.J. was waving in the rest of the detectives. I was shocked when I saw a blonde lady, who I would later learn was Christie Prody, in the room. She had a striking resemblance to what I remembered from pictures of Nicole Brown. It was a creepy moment that I will never forget.

After inviting everyone in, Simpson asked Prody and another lady to leave so he could talk with us. Prody left a small dog in the suite.

I made my way into the living area of the suite where there was a bed, some chairs and a couch. The living area was sunken and separated from the entrance by a few steps. There was a bar area by the entrance, where a few of the surveillance detectives stayed, and a nook or kitchen area off of the main living area. His suite was big and nice. I grabbed a chair at the foot of the bed and turned it toward the bed. Rod did the same. Linda sat on a chair toward the head of the bed on the side farthest from the main entrance. Eddie came over by us. I didn't pay much attention to where the rest of the surveillance detectives were. I introduced myself and O.J. made sure to tell me again that his lawyer was on his way and we would need to wait for him to talk about the incident at the Palace Station. Simpson sat down at the foot of the bed and I started talking with him to build a rapport.

I started asking Simpson conversational questions about what brought him to Las Vegas and where he lives. Linda was sitting out of Simpson's immediate sight, taking diligent notes. Simpson said he had come to Las Vegas for the wedding of his friend, Tom Scotto, from Florida. As time went on, Simpson's behavior became erratic and his speech pattern and body movements seemed fast. He was very talkative. Based on my training and experience, Simpson was exhibiting signs of being under the influence of controlled substances. There is no way for me to say for sure, but his behavior was consistent with someone who uses cocaine or methamphetamine.

Simpson made many unsolicited incriminating statements as he talked with me, and Linda was there to write them all down without him noticing. As he talked, he decided to call his attorney to see where his attorney was. When there was no answer, O.J. left a message. What happened next was one of the strangest moments of my contact with Simpson. He set his phone down between his legs while sitting on the bed and his dog jumped on his lap for a moment. The dog jumped down and ran off somewhere in the room. Simpson continued talking for a few moments and then stopped with a look of panic on his face. He didn't stand up, but he started looking around where he was sitting and after 10 to 15 seconds of uncomfortable silence, he began talking to himself asking, "Where's my phone?" After a few moments, he asked me if I did something with his phone, which caught me a little off guard. Eddie joined in the conversation and bluntly said, "O.J., your phone is between your legs." Simpson still had a panicked look on his face as he looked down. When he saw his phone, he started to smile. He grabbed the phone with both his hands and started to giggle. Simpson lay back on his bed with his feet still on the floor and started wiggling side to side while holding his phone on his chest. This went on for approximately 30 seconds, which seemed like an eternity as I sat there and watched it unfold. He sat back up as if nothing happened and continued talking with me. It's hard to talk with people who are displaying this kind of inconsistent behavior because their mind spits out random thoughts and changes the direction of the conversation repeatedly. During our conversation, Linda took the following notes:

*He's the guy who called me. Referring to Riccio, a person of interest in our investigation.*

*These guys are afraid cause of the Turnover orders. Referring to the victims, Beardsley and Fromong having to turn over any O.J. Simpson memorabilia to the California courts because of a civil matter.*

*The guys left in two cars. Referring to the other males who went to the Palace Station with Mr. Simpson during the incident. Mr. Simpson said the males, including himself, left in two separate cars.*

*I didn't care about the memorabilia, I wanted the family stuff. Referring to the items taken from the Palace Station room during the incident.*

*These guys know me. Referring to the victims Beardsley and Fromong.*

*First I hear we broke in ... then it was an armed robbery.*

*Referring to the media reports that were upsetting to him.*

*If these guys were legit, they would have got big bucks on the Internet. Referring to the victims being able to sell property taken in the incident.*

*They sneakin'. Referring to the victim's activities with the memorabilia.*

*I forgot about this stuff. Referring to the memorabilia.*

*Riccio faxed me over the list. Referring to the list of memorabilia that would be for sale.*

*I didn't know what they had. Referring to the memorabilia that would be in the Palace Station hotel room.*

*I wanted them to go into the room and see if it was my stuff and call me. Referring to the males that went with Mr. Simpson to the Palace Station hotel room where the memorabilia was displayed.*

*Riccio was a good guy. Referring to Thomas Riccio.*

*It's bullshit. Referring to Michael Gilbert being his ex-manager.*

*I never had a real manager, I had lawyers. Referring to persons claiming to be Mr. Simpson's managers or ex-managers.*

*It wasn't about that being physical. Referring to what was to occur in the Palace Station hotel room.*

*I told them I cannot believe you guys did this shit. Referring to what Mr. Simpson said to victims in the Palace*

*Station hotel room during the incident.*

*Beardsley is certifiable.* Referring to victim Alfred Beardsley.

*You know what lawyers are like.* Referring to trying to get hold of his lawyer on the phone.

*I will tell you this, I tried to call Riccio.* Referring to calling Thomas Riccio after the incident.

*I didn't look at the stuff, I saw the balls down in the car.* Referring to the items taken from the room and put into a car after the incident.

*I think they only brought some of the stuff, it wasn't all there.* Referring to the items in the Palace Station room not being everything the victims had.

*My All American ball! I would never give that away! They were all sitting on the bed. I would never give Mike this stuff.* Referring to a specific football on the bed inside the Palace Station room.

*I told him I could talk but my lawyer said 'No Juice'.* Referring to talking to his lawyer.

*Here is what pisses me off! I saw Riccio on TV but they keep putting on the bad stuff.* Referring to an interview Thomas Riccio gave to the media.

*Armed robbery! I knew I was going to be hearing from the cops.* Referring to what Mr. Simpson heard on TV.

*As pissed off as I was with them, it wasn't that type of*

*thing. Referring to the incident being a crime.*

*They said 'Take it' ... 'We cool Juice' ... 'We cool O.J.' Referring to what the victims said to Mr. Simpson during the incident.*

*Everyone there can corroborate the story. Referring to what happened in the Palace Station hotel room.*

*The guy was going to be the guy pretending to buy my stuff. Referring to a white male that was with Mr. Simpson during the incident (shown in a picture).*

*Why are they not in trouble? Referring to the victims not being arrested.*

*Where did they get the stuff? Referring to where the victims gained the memorabilia.*
*They didn't claim they got it legitimate?!! Referring to if the victims said they legally owned the memorabilia.*

*I don't have nothing. Referring to Mr. Simpson not having police reports for the memorabilia.*

*So when they come up, I know (they're) not in a warehouse. Referring to Mr. Simpson not knowing where his property is and sometimes seeing his property for sale as memorabilia.*

*Riccio said they faxed him a list ... everything wasn't there. Referring to what items were in the Palace Station hotel room and what items were on a list of what would be there.*

*I didn't take the time to go through it. Referring to Mr. Simpson not looking through the property taken from the*

*Palace Station hotel room.*

*Bruce said take the stuff and go. Referring to what victim Fromong said to Mr. Simpson during the incident.*

*I guess they had Joe Montana lithos. Referring to lithographs displayed in the Palace Station hotel room and taken during the incident.*

Simpson's statements were not responses to questions; they were random statements he made to questions as simple as asking why he was in Las Vegas. There is a general rule about interviewing talkative suspects of just letting them talk, which I did not stick to here. After about 45 minutes of listening to his rambling and oftentimes jumbled conversation, I ended the contact. It is always better to listen and let a suspect talk because it provides more information to work with later. We were tired and he clearly was not going to allow me to conduct a traditional interview without his attorney present. He had given me enough in his random statements to help with the investigation and connect some of the loose ends, such as confirming Riccio's involvement. I gave Simpson my business card with my phone number and asked him to call me when he got in touch with his lawyer if they then wanted to talk again. I thanked him for his time. Simpson shook all of our hands as we walked toward the door of his suite.

We walked back to the elevator where the security guard who had escorted us up was still waiting for us. The surveillance squad resumed its assignment, which was no longer covert. After we got down to the main floor, Eddie, Rod, Linda and I debriefed our contact with Simpson. Linda went over the notes she had taken and we discussed Simpson's odd behavior. It was about 3 p.m. on Friday the 14th and Rod released us for the day, instructing us to report back for duty on Saturday for our regularly scheduled shift starting at 3 p.m. I had spoken with my wife a few times throughout the night and day and she decided it would be safer for her to get me a hotel room in Vegas for the night rather than making the hour-long drive home after that long of a shift. She booked me a room at Planet Hollywood, which worked out for her, too, because she drove into Vegas with our daughters to let them swim at the pool. By the time I got to Planet Hollywood, she had already checked in and taken fresh clothes up to the room for me. She met me in the lobby and handed me the key, then she and the girls went to the pool.

# CHAPTER 5
# WALTER ALEXANDER

On Saturday morning, two days after the robbery at the Palace Station, I woke up refreshed after a hard night's sleep. I looked at my phone and noticed I had a few voicemails. I called to check my messages and the first one I missed was from Simpson. He called me at 7:30 p.m. on Sept. 14, which would have been approximately six hours after I left his suite at the Palms. Simpson's message was:

*Uh, hey, uh, Officer Caldwell, uh, this is O.J. calling. Uh, yes my lawyer is taking your numbers, is interested in calling you late tonight or early in the morning um, uh, to set up this, uh, interview. He also said that he will endeavor to get all the guys that we have, to get their statement. But two of the guys I really don't know. Uh, uh, I talked to two of the guys already and they said yeah, they'll, they're willing to give, ready and willing to give their statements. The other two guys, uh, I really don't know. Um, but, um, uh, so he ... you I will give him both your cards, OK? Uh, hope all is well and sorry about of this crap that you're ... (laughing) you take care.*

His message caught me a little off guard for a couple of reasons. My first thought was to question why he was calling me if his attorney was going to call later and then my second thought was to question why Simpson was being over-the-top friendly telling me, "Hope all is well and sorry about of this crap that you're ... (laughing) you take care." I was left thinking that either his attorney was lazy or O.J. was ignoring the advice from his lawyer because no attorney worth anything would tell their client to talk to the police without them being present.

I believe Simpson's over-the-top friendliness in the message he left me was symptomatic of psychological issues that are deeper than I can fully understand. Though I might not fully understand what is going on in his head, I have experienced criminals exhibiting this kind of behavior in other circumstances. At one point in my career, I had the opportunity to serve as a resident officer in a rural community of Clark County. During that time, I got to see a remarkable contrast between the fast-paced and action-packed policing of Las Vegas to the intimate and deliberate policing of a town where everyone knows the police officers and where the officers and their families are actively involved in the community. In this setting, it was easier for me to notice patterns that I never had the time to consider in the fast pace of other assignments I had with the LVMPD.

There were simple patterns that surfaced, like how rare it was to have a kid with two parents and a stay-at-home mom to get into trouble that required police involvement (that is not to say kids without stay-at-home moms will get into trouble, just that in my experience the ones who do get into trouble often don't have a traditional family structure). Other noticeable patterns surfaced as well: it was rare for an adult to be arrested who did not have a tattoo or who causally drinks alcohol (again I am not saying all people with tattoos or who occasionally drink alcohol get arrested, just that most who do get arrested embrace those cultural activities).

There is also a noticeable difference between how adult and children criminals act when they are involved in criminal activity or when they have been caught for a crime they have committed. When children are caught red-handed committing or having committed a crime, they often act like they have disappointed the parents; they suddenly want to be friendly, they want you to think they are not bad and to give them value apart from the crime they committed. They become concerned with wanting to be your friend and they often shift into a role of being overly helpful in solving the crime as if their friendly helpfulness will reshape your view of them and you will be a little less disappointed in them.

In this case, Simpson is a grown man who was caught red-handed and the more I got to think about his phone message, the more I likened him to having a childlike mentality of thinking he could smooth over his crimes with a smile and childlike small talk as if to say, "Aw, shucks, did I do that?"

I didn't have the time to put much thought into the voicemail Simpson left me. I knew I had a busy day ahead of me. As I was getting ready to head into work, I turned on the TV and Simpson's involvement in a robbery at the Palace Station was still taking up a considerable amount of time on the news networks. I knew from previous cases that had received local attention that the more attention a case gets on the news, the more involved the public would be in helping to provide information they think will help.

I didn't need to be at work until 3 p.m., but I figured I could get a jump on the day by going in early. I left the hotel on the strip at about 6:30 a.m. and headed toward my office. The Las Vegas Strip is an interesting place in the morning. There are people out jogging on the sidewalks in front of the casinos, the street sweepers are out, and the road construction crews are busily getting work done before the bulk of the guests are up and moving. It is a peaceful time considering the party atmosphere of Las Vegas. I turned my radio to our local talk radio station and the O.J. Simpson robbery was the topic of discussion. I listened and they were already creating the false narrative of O.J. just taking property back that belonged to him. I didn't give it much thought because it did not match the details I had learned up to this point.

At the robbery office, the day shift robbery squad also was coming in. I had been in the robbery section longer than all but five of the detectives assigned to the section, so I knew most of the other detectives pretty well. The first detective I saw as I came into the office was a good friend of mine, Scott Kavon. Scott instantly started in on me about how much I owe him and how I was lucky that he was willing to do so much work on my case. I had no idea what he was talking about, but I knew it was something good and he was going to bust my chops for a while, so I might as well sit back and take it. Scott's partner was Det. Mark Gregory. As Scott was doing everything he could to build up how he knew something important but he wasn't quite ready to tell me yet, Mark walked up behind him with a file in his hand.

Mark and Scott were both senior detectives who had worked together for years in the robbery section and then for years before that in the vice section. The LVMPD vice section is the unit primarily responsible for investigating sex-work related crimes in Las Vegas and Clark County. Mark and Scott were the two guys I would go to when I needed help or guidance. They were the guys in the office who were leaders without being supervisors.

As Mark walked up, he had a pretty big smile on his face. He undoubtedly heard Scott and I think under normal circumstances would have joined in, but I also think he knew he had good information and he wanted to get moving on it. Mark and Scott were working late on the 14th. At about 10 p.m., Mark was contacted by an LVMPD dispatcher who told him she had a woman on the line with information about the O.J. Simpson robbery. The woman refused to give the dispatcher her name or phone number, so Mark had the dispatcher transfer the call to him. The woman continued to refuse to identify herself to Mark, but did say she had known O.J. Simpson and Nicole Brown and that she was going through a divorce during the time Simpson was on trial for Nicole Brown and Ron Goldman's murders. Mark noted the woman explained how after the murder she became enraged with Simpson, believing that he committed the murders. She was also resentful of the lifestyle he continued to live. There is a common saying that I have found considerable truth in: "Hell has no fury like a woman scorned." Upset wives, girlfriends, ex-wives, and ex-girlfriends oftentimes have great information and can be great sources of information. There is a balance in understanding that sometimes, scorned women will overexaggerate and will make things up just to get the source of their frustration in trouble. So their information requires independent verification to make sure it is not just a witch-hunt.

The anonymous caller told Mark that one of the men involved in the robbery with O.J. Simpson was Walter Alexander and she even knew his date of birth. Somehow, the anonymous caller knew Alexander was due to leave Las Vegas on Sept. 15 at 12:35 p.m. on Southwest Airlines Flight 2981 to Phoenix, Ariz. Alexander provided the guns for the robbery and he would know all of the people involved, the woman said.

The information the anonymous caller provided seemed too specific to be made up. After getting off the phone, Mark and Scott went to work on verifying the information she provided. Scott contacted Southwest Airlines and confirmed there was a Walter Alexander scheduled to be on Flight 2981 out of Las Vegas to Phoenix, just as the caller had reported. Southwest Airlines provided the home address used by Walter Alexander to book his plane ticket. From there, Scott and Mark were able to get more identifying information about Alexander. Alexander had driver's license records in both California and Arizona, but Mark and Scott were unable to get a picture of Alexander at that time. All of the information the woman had provided had checked out up to that point. By the next morning, prior to me coming to the office, Mark was able to get a driver's license photo of Walter Alexander and he clearly was one of the suspects who could be seen in the surveillance video. There were other tips that had come in and were on my desk waiting for me, but none were as solid as this one. I called Eddie and told him we had a lead and asked if he could come in early so we could follow up on it. While Eddie was on his way in, Mark and Scott continued to work on researching biographical information about Alexander and I went to work on completing paperwork. I called Sgt. Pete Rossi, who was the supervisor at Las Vegas'

McCarran International Airport, to see what resources he had available to help us locate Alexander.

Sgt. Rossi had been at the department for one year longer than I had and we worked together on two separate assignments. When I finished my police academy and completed my required training, I was assigned to the Southwest Area Command as a patrol officer on graveyard. In the late '90s, the LVMPD was a fast-growing department, which equated to fast promotions to detective and movement to specialized units. It also meant a large number of rookie officers working graveyard with very few senior officers to mentor new officers. So many of us were in our early 20s, and the 24-year-old with two years of experience as a police officer was the senior guy everyone looked to. Pete was one of those officers for me. Pete was also my first friend to be shot in the line of duty. One night, we had just finished graveyard briefing and all the graveyard officers, including Pete, started their regular patrol duties. Officer Fred Castle and I were assigned to bike patrol that night, so we both got into a black-and-white patrol car and drove to Clark High School, where the bike office for the Southwest Area Command was located. Fred and I got our police bicycles from the office and started our shift from there. Bike patrol was something we would get to do a couple times a month, so when we checked out our bicycles from the office, we normally took them out to the parking lot and rode around for a few minutes to acclimate ourselves to the bicycles. After a few minutes of riding down some steps and going over some curbs, we were all set to go. It was getting close to midnight and we needed to head over to our assigned area if we wanted to catch some drug traffic before it got too late. Between 11 p.m. and midnight, there was a swing shift and graveyard shift overlap, so the radio traffic was heavy on our police radios and it was hard to track what everyone was doing in the area command. As we headed south, I heard officers get dispatched to an armed robbery at a Mexican restaurant at

Sahara and Decatur, which was a 10-minute bicycle ride in the opposite direction. There were multiple units assigned and more units were not needed, so Fred and I kept heading toward our assigned area. Within a few moments of being dispatched, I heard an officer broadcast he had arrived at the reported robbery. The next bit of radio traffic came out fast and was hard to understand, but it was clear enough to know Pete had just been shot. Listening to the dispatcher trying to get more information was hard because Pete was not answering. As Fred and I turn back to the bike office to get our black-and-white patrol vehicle, I heard the sirens of police cars turn on all around us and within moments, I saw speeding patrol units with their emergency lights and sirens on rushing to help Pete. The suspects had shot Pete in the face as they came out of the business and as Pete went down, the suspects fled the area. The suspects were caught and prosecuted, but it was the last night I worked with Pete for years. I eventually made detective and was transferred to the robbery section, where we again worked together for the next three years until Pete was promoted to a sergeant.

When I called Pete to ask if there was anything he could do to help, he had an instant idea. He told me he was going to call Southwest Airlines and have them change Alexander's ticket status to one that would require him to come to the ticket desk. McCarren International Airport is one of the largest and busiest airports in the nation and there are a few ways for a person to check in and go straight to the TSA security check area. We could just wait for him at the gate for his flight, but Pete's way made everything so much easier.

I called Eddie and asked him to go directly to the airport and meet us there. Scott, Mark and I left the robbery office and headed to the airport. We arrived early, but that was good because it gave me a few minutes to survey the area and find good places to observe people coming and going from the Southwest Airlines ticket counter.

Scott, Mark, and I walked upstairs above the ticketing

counters and to the police substation; Eddie already was there talking with Pete. It was only 10 a.m., so we had a few minutes to sit in the empty briefing room and come up with a plan. It only took a few minutes to create a plan, so we sat around and visited while we waited. Visiting with other cops in a work environment always makes for a freewheeling conversation. Briefing rooms are a safe place for us—a place we don't have to always be looking over our shoulder for someone walking up behind us; it is one of the most relaxed places for police officers on duty. This is when the funny stories are told. Over the years, I have learned that people who are not police officers enjoy stories about how a crook was caught, what the details of the crime were and what's going to happen to the bad guy next. Cops enjoy the funny stories. Cops enjoy stories about other cops making mistakes and we love to give each other a hard time. And when it comes to a funny mistake, we have an elephant's memory. So when a robbery detective and his partner are chasing a bank robbery suspect and while they initiate a completely righteous technique where the front bumper of the police car is used to push either side of the suspect vehicle's rear bumper to one side or another causing the suspect's car to spin out of control, at the same time the suspect was going to dive out of his moving vehicle. It's not the bank robbery, the pursuit or the driving technique that is worthy of retelling among other cops. As the suspect started to drive at the same time the detective's vehicle began to push the rear of the suspect vehicle to the right, the momentum of the suspect's vehicle spinning around caused the bad guy to launch out into the path of the detective's vehicle and before he could stop, they ran over the suspect. In a moment of panic, the detectives thought the car was on top of the suspect. The driver put the car in reverse to back off the suspect, so they could render aid and they ran him over again. It's important to note the suspect lived and is in prison, but that kind of story lives for years and cops bring it up to give other cops a hard time.

At about 11:20 a.m., all five of us set up in surveillance positions around the Southwest Airlines ticket desk and the closest entrance. Pete was in his uniform, so he kept the farthest distance away from the immediate area. At 11:58 a.m., Eddie spotted Alexander at the curbside check. The Southwest Airlines employees did not know we were looking for Alexander, so to them, there was just a random issue with the ticket requiring him to be directed to the main ticketing counter. As Eddie watched the employee explain to Alexander that he needed to go inside, Eddie called me to tell me Alexander was about to be coming in the entrance. Eddie followed Alexander as I walked toward them while he was still outside of the entrance by the curbside check-in. When I was about 20 feet away from Alexander, I reached up to my neck to pull my hang badge out of my shirt. I kept my eyes on Alexander and there was no doubt in my mind he saw me pull my badge out and knew I was coming for him. I had watched the surveillance video from the Palace Station multiple times and looked at the still pictures of the suspects printed from the surveillance video; I had no doubt the man I was approaching was one of the suspects with O.J. Simpson during the armed robbery. He was pulling a large luggage bag behind him and he slowed down, anticipating my contact. We were just outside the entrance doors before we both stopped walking. I said, "How are you sir? My name is Detective Caldwell with the Las Vegas Metropolitan Police Department. Can I talk to you for a moment?" Alexander responded, saying that he was willing to talk with me. I motioned for Alexander to follow me and walked just inside the entrance where there was a little more room. I stopped there and asked if I could see some form of identification. He reached into his back pocket and pulled out his wallet. As he opened his wallet, I could see his driver's license bearing the name "Walter Alexander" behind a clear plastic flap. He was still holding the handle of his luggage and I asked him,

"Would you like to know why I want to talk with you?" He quickly replied, "You mean the O.J. thing?" I told him that I would like to know more about what happened and asked if he would be willing to follow us up to an office to talk some more. He said, "Yeah, let's go to the office." He could have said no, but based on what I knew at this point, I would have just arrested him. I walked next to him and reached for the handle of his luggage. He automatically let it go and I took the handle into my hand then led him toward the Airport Substation.

There were many things to consider about how I was going to approach my interview. I have found it is always better to try to make suspects feel like they are cooperating and that they have some control of their circumstances— even if they don't. I have also found it is good to let suspects know that I am not talking to them for just some random fishing expedition, that my contacting them is deliberate and I already know the details I am about to ask about. While we were walking up to the substation, I told Alexander he was free to leave, but no matter what he did, I was going to seize his luggage pending a search warrant. No, he was not free to leave, but I wanted him to feel like he had some options. As we walked into the airport substation, I had not mentioned the robbery and simply asked if he would give me consent to search his bag. In a case like this, I would not accept his consent because I felt he could later argue he only gave me consent due to him being surrounded by detectives or because he was at the airport where he might feel that if he did not cooperate he could lose his ability to fly out of Las Vegas that day. Even though I planned on getting a search warrant for his bag, I asked for his consent because I wanted to see how he responded. He said, "The memorabilia isn't in my bag." Eddie quickly added that we were looking for a suit, too. He never responded to my question about giving me consent to search his bag. I led Alexander into the briefing room, where we both sat down at a table. One prong of the Miranda requirement had been met because even though I told him he was free to leave, there is no way a reasonable person would think they could just walk away at this point. But I have not yet asked him about a crime, so the second prong has not been met and therefore, Miranda is not yet applicable. I pulled out the surveillance picture I used to help me spot him, pointed to him and said, "This is the suit we are looking for." He looked at me and told me it was in the bag. I was sitting on the end of the table and Alexander was sitting to my right. I told him I would like to ask him some questions about the night of the robbery and, just as I was about to advise him of his Miranda rights, he asked to call his attorney.

A suspect's request for an attorney brings all the momentum of an interview to a screeching halt, except Alexander said he wanted to help, but needed to talk to his attorney first. I made sure Alexander was in a safe area that provided him privacy to talk with his attorney and walked away. Within five minutes, he was done with his call and called for me. His attorney directed him not to talk with me until he had a deal in place and to not give me consent to search his bag. I would not have expected anything different from a defense lawyer. At this point, I advised Alexander he was under arrest for armed robbery, burglary with a firearm and kidnapping with the use of a firearm.

I still had to advise District Attorney Roger I was about to make an arrest in the case and tell him the suspect was willing to cooperate if he had a deal in place. It was Saturday, so I called Roger on his cell phone and told him what I had. When I asked if he was willing to work out a deal, he asked where Alexander's attorney was located. I told him the lawyer was in California and that Alexander was able to reach him on his cell phone. Roger seemed pretty excited at the prospect of getting more details from one of the suspects, said he was on his way to the robbery office and would meet us there. I escorted Alexander out to my unmarked vehicle and we all drove back to the robbery office. We had some small talk on the way back to the office, but overall, it was a pretty quiet ride.

# CHAPTER 6
# WALTER TALKS

I arrived back at the robbery office at about 1 p.m. Eddie pulled in right behind me and we walked Alexander up to the third floor where our office was. On Saturdays, the building is not open to the public and there were only a few units that worked seven days a week; the robbery section was one of those units. The robbery section shared the third floor of the building with the homicide section whose detectives only came in on the weekend when they had a murder to work on or when they had immediate follow-up that needed to be done. We shared our interview rooms with homicide, so Saturdays were a good day to bring suspects in because the interview rooms were usually empty. The interview rooms also doubled as holding cells. We walked Alexander to an interview room and left him in the room, which was monitored by cameras. Eddie brought the luggage up to the office, wheeled it to my desk and waited for me there. When I made it to my desk, my cell phone rang. It was Roger, who was at the main entrance to our office building and needed to be let in.

As I approached the main entrance, I could see through the glass doors as Roger stood in shorts and a T-shirt holding a leather-bound notebook. As I unlocked the door, Roger greeted me with a smile and a handshake. I didn't know him well enough yet to make fun of him showing up in his gym clothes, but I wanted to. We rode the elevator up to the third floor and on the way up, I filled him in with as much detail as I could about my perception of Alexander. Little observations about a person's personality help to establish plans for interviews and, in this case, negotiations. To me, Alexander acted like an old wannabe pimp who was overly concerned about how he looked and how others viewed him.

He seemed like the kind of guy who would do anything to stay out of prison.

Roger asked me to take him to our conference room and if we had a speakerphone so he could call Alexander's lawyer. I brought him into the robbery office conference room, which was the same room we conducted our briefings in, but we didn't have a phone in the room. I think Roger was a little disappointed in the facilities we had to offer, yet he was flexible enough to say a cell phone on speaker would work fine, too. I got Alexander from the interview room and brought him to the conference room. This initial meeting was to just get information for Roger to contact Alexander's attorney to begin working out an agreement that would allow Alexander to talk with me.

I had removed Alexander's handcuffs and introduced him to Roger, who was on the backside of the large conference room table. Roger stood up when we came in the room and, after I made the introductions, motioned for Alexander to sit down across the table from him. I found it very significant that Roger did not extend his hand to offer a handshake to Alexander. We all recognized the importance of getting information from Alexander, but he was also still a man who was just involved in committing an armed robbery and did not deserve to be treated like an upstanding member of our community.

I knew how important this meeting was and also how rare it was. I had been a police officer for almost 10 years at that point and I had never heard of the district attorney coming in on a Saturday to work out an arrangement to get a suspect's statement. For as much as I wanted to treat this like any other case to avoid the appearance of going the extra mile to just convict O.J. Simpson, the reality was that this was going to be like no other case I have ever worked. Because O.J. Simpson was involved, I was going to have to go the extra mile to get real justice.

There was a case I worked while I was a robbery

detective that always bothered me because I could not do more. It involved a series of five business robberies in which three to four young men would enter a cell phone store in the middle of the day. Armed with handguns, they would order all of the customers into a bathroom or back office, take all of the products and money they could get their hands on and within minutes, they were gone. During some of the robberies, customers and employees were pistol-whipped for no reason. The victims were just average, everyday individuals and families who were in the wrong place at the wrong time. When the first robbery of this series happened, I thought there was no way this was going to prove to only be a one-time crime. It is hard to put into words the terror the victims of a crime like this go through. In talking to the victims, I observed a broad range of emotions from fearful crying to pride-filled anger. It hurts to see people have to go through this kind of experience, but I had little evidence to go on after the first robbery. The victims saw the suspects' faces and said they could identify them if they saw them again, but the description they provided matched tens of thousands of young men in the Las Vegas valley. When the second one happened, I got sick to my stomach because there was not much more to go on and it confirmed my feeling that the suspects were not going to stop until they were caught. More victims terrorized, more people experiencing the trauma of just going about your daily shopping and then monsters armed with guns come into your life to steal more than the cash in your wallet, but your sense of security and peace. They were the same suspects and now I had a vague vehicle description of a dark SUV. I would have loved to have unlimited resources to devote to these robberies, but other crime does not stop and as a robbery detective, I had other active cases I had to work also. With the third robbery, the suspects started beating the victims. The violent nature of these crimes was increasing fast and happening about once a week. On the third robbery, one witness got a license plate number. The SUV was stolen, which gave me more information to gather and more places to look for information leading to the suspects' identification. Each consecutive robbery gave me more information to work with, but there is an undeniable feeling of responsibility when another robbery happened and I had not yet stopped them. A day after the fifth robbery, a patrol officer spotted the suspect vehicle parked unoccupied in a residential neighborhood in the northern part of the valley. A few of my partners and I set up around the vehicle in unmarked cars—where we could not be seen—and sure enough, at about 7 a.m., came a young man with a backpack who matched the description of one of the suspects. We rushed him and took him into custody right before he got into the stolen vehicle. The vehicle contained some of the stolen property from the robberies. He was heading to school for the day. Once I had him in custody, I took him home; the suspect invoked his Miranda rights and, with the support of his parents, refused to cooperate. He wanted a lawyer and a deal. He is just one of hundreds of thugs who were going to be arrested that day and the system was not about to slow down for him wanting a deal to help identify the other suspects he had hurt so many people with. It would have been nice to have a prosecutor come meet with me at the office and work with this suspect's attorney to facilitate the suspect telling me who the other suspects were. I knew once one was caught, the series would stop and it did, but now, it was going to take many days of additional work to establish other possible suspects.

As Alexander settled in, Roger called Alexander's attorney. An agreement like this is not like most people would think. The prosecution does not offer a free pass for information, which makes sense when you stop and think about it. The agreement basically says Alexander will provide the police with a full and honest statement that cannot be used against him if there is no agreeable plea deal after his statement is verified. This prevents a deal being put in place for a suspect who is just a peripheral player and offers no added value with the information he can provide. We all knew that Alexander had information that would clear up what led up to the armed robbery and what happened during the armed robbery. There is a gamble in offering a suspect the opportunity to give a statement about a case. The gamble for the investigative side is if a suspect is guilty of a serious crime and honest, there is an obligation to still make a deal. The gamble for the other side is that if the suspect doesn't like the deal or isn't honest, the statement can only be used to impeach false testimony. Alexander wanted specifics about what kind of deal he was going to get, but Roger stayed firm in saying he does not work that way. First, Alexander had to tell us what he knew and then they would talk about what kind of deal there was to be had. "The first horse to the trough gets the cleanest water," Roger said, which provided a moment of levity because Alexander had no idea what David was talking. I had to take a moment to explain that the first person to talk would get the best deal. Alexander and his attorney agreed to the terms offered by Roger, who began to draw up some legal paperwork. While the paperwork was being completed, I took Alexander back to one of the interview rooms.

Once Alexander's lawyer and the district attorney had completed their communication, it was time to start the interview. Roger wanted to stay for the interview, which was the first time I had ever experienced a prosecutor sitting in on an interview; he did make it clear that he would only be observing and not participating in the interview. Because Roger wanted to observe, I decided it was best to conduct the interview in the conference room to allow for more room. I was about to interview a suspect about a crime that was already getting national attention and even though it was not a complex crime, the crime did have more variables involved than a normal armed robbery and kidnapping. Interviews get more complex when there are multiple unidentified suspects and multiple victims. In this case, I had the curveball of Riccio, who in my opinion was teetering between being a co-conspiring suspect or a witness who knew something was going to happen but was not smart enough to see that he lit a fuse to a powder keg. Though I was going to conduct the interview with Eddie, I thought it would be wise to have an extra set of ears in the room to help pick up on anything Eddie or I might miss, which is why I asked Scott to sit in.

I started my digital recorder and conducted a short preamble noting the date, time, location and who was in the room. In a situation like this, I felt the best thing I could do was to let Alexander tell his story and then I would formulate my questions as we went along.

Alexander settled into his chair as if he were preparing for a performance he knew everyone else in the room was dying to hear and began to tell us what happened starting from the morning of the armed robbery. Alexander had flown to Las Vegas that morning to attend a friend's wedding, Scotto, a mutual friend of Simpson's. Alexander made it clear he was a longtime personal friend of Simpson and even knew Simpson's children.

Spencer, another friend of Alexander's who lived in Las Vegas, picked him up at the airport. Though Alexander consistently referred to this friend as Spencer, Spencer was later identified as Michael McClinton. While they were driving to McClinton's house, Alexander received a call from another friend he referred to as C.J., later identified as Clarence Stewart. Stewart, who also was friends with Simpson, told Alexander that Simpson wanted to talk with him. Alexander said he tried to get hold of Simpson on the phone, but he couldn't. He knew Simpson was staying at the Palms Resort, so they drove over to see what Simpson needed. I don't think Alexander recognized that everyone else in the room was trained and experienced in statement analysis and, as we listened to his story, we also know there was good evidence in the small details. As he began telling his side of what happened, I have already picked up on the fact that when O.J. wants something, Alexander does what O.J. wants.

At the Palms, Simpson told Alexander and McClinton about these guys in Vegas having property that belonged to Simpson. Simpson told them it was "my memorabilia" and a guy named Tom Ricci (Riccio) told Simpson where the memorabilia was and he had set up a meeting with the guys who possessed what Simpson said was his. During this meeting, Alexander explained, Simpson asked if they had guns that they could bring to "look tough." Simpson wanted the people who he felt had his property to know "we're here for business." McClinton offered up that he did have some guns, but they were out at his house. They needed to get the guns and would meet back up with Simpson later.

There are certain verbal red flags I listen for when suspects are giving a statement. I find that when they are talking about something they think might get them in more trouble, might be morally wrong by their own standards or they just want to cover up, they will use certain phrases. An example of this was frequently seen on the sitcom "Seinfeld" with the expression "yadda yadda yadda." A more realistic and commonly used expression I've heard as a robbery detective was "whoopty woo woo." As an example, an armed robbery suspect might confess to the crime with an oversimplified statement such as: "I walked up to the lady and whoopty woo woo, then I ran out the doors." The suspect does not want to say he pointed a gun in the face of a lady and demanded money. He wants to skip that detail and just hopes no one will ask specific details about it.

As Alexander begins to tell us about the guns, his version of euphemizing surfaced in the expression "you know." Suddenly, he is saying "you know" multiple times in one sentence, which is an instant red flag for me. Alexander said, "So, *you know*, we were running late, *you know*, they had to keep putting it off, *you know*, because, um, he (Simpson) wanted us to come. My friend, uh, Spencer, um, had a, *you know*, he had a, had his gun and, um, he asked me, um, *you know*, he said, *you know*, here's a .22." His sudden overuse of "you know" points me to think he knew what he did was wrong in going to get the gun and now that he was caught, he was uncomfortable with admitting he had a gun. He probably did not want me to know he wanted to have a gun. To an investigator, Alexander had just unwittingly provided me with more insight into who he is. O.J. wanted to talk with him, so he sought O.J. out. O.J. wanted guns, so he got a gun. He did whatever O.J. wanted.

As Alexander began describing meeting Simpson at the Palace Station, his use of the phrase "you know" continued at an unusually high rate. Alexander and McClinton met with Simpson and Stewart, the two other suspects and Riccio in the lobby of the hotel. Alexander said Riccio "had set everything up so, you know, but he was acting like he didn't, you know, that he was just bringing a buyer." Riccio told them to follow him to Room 1203. There was an interesting shift in Alexander's explanation and the focus of his blame as he began to describe what happened when they entered the room. He made McClinton out to be the primary aggressor, claiming he never pulled the gun he was carrying out of his waistband. "Spencer (McClinton), when he walked in, you know, he saw several guys and he kinda just, you know, kinda just got a little bit too feisty, you know. I mean, Juice had told him just to carry the gun, not to, you know, take it out, just to show it but now he brought the gun out as was like, you know, up against the walls, you know, type situation." After this, he told me—and tried to reassure me—that he never pulled the gun out of his waistband. I'm sure in his mind, he was doing damage control for himself by painting McClinton out to be a mad man waving a gun around and he was the controlled one who did not pull his out. His efforts to minimize his actions were pointless for me. It is not relevant if he showed the gun or pointed the gun—all that matters was that he had the gun and the victims saw it. On a separate level, the victims were consistent with their story that the two suspects with the guns had the guns in their hands.

Alexander provided some details as to what happened in Room 1203. He described the victims being surprised when Simpson walked into the room and continued to describe McClinton being aggressive toward the victims. He described Simpson talking with the victims and then McClinton telling the victims to put their phones on the bed so they wouldn't call the police. He described quickly gathering up all of the memorabilia in the room and then leaving. Alexander took one of the phones and claimed that after they had left the room, Simpson told him to go back and give it to the victim. Alexander went back, but could not remember which room they were in, so he kept the phone. This was another subtle indication that when O.J. Simpson told Alexander to jump, Alexander jumped.

It was important for me to remember that prior to this interview, O.J. Simpson had left a message on my cell phone mentioning that he had already talked to some of the other guys who were involved and they were ready to give statements. I needed to be aware there was probably some discussion among the suspects about what they should and should not say to me when I interviewed them.

As Alexander started to talk about the property that was stolen, the "you know" phrase again started to surface. It was again clear this was an area where did not want to talk about specific details. He mentioned having the victim's sunglasses, cell phone and Joe Montana memorabilia, which they all knew did not belong to Simpson. He claimed that he and the other suspects discussed getting all the property that did not belong to Simpson back to the victims. Even though he explained they had a desire to return some of the property, he also said they knew the police were called and they knew they needed to "get rid of this stuff." They loaded all of the stolen property into Stewart's Lincoln Navigator. Alexander said Stewart hid everything.

As Alexander described some property not being Simpson's, he also described other property they stole as belonging to Simpson. I asked what made him think any of the property belonged to Simpson. He said it was all stuff Simpson had signed. When I asked if it was possible for other people to own things Simpson had signed, he did acknowledge that as a possibility in a way that caused me to think he had not considered that option before. He recognized Fromong from years ago when he and Simpson worked together. Alexander was convinced Fromong had stolen some of the property from Simpson and was selling it.

There was shift in Alexander's overarching theme up to this point. Before, he seemed to point his finger at McClinton as the bad guy and now, he shifted to pointing to Simpson as the bad guy. When the interview started to focus of the stolen property, Alexander said:

"O.J. felt like he could just come and take his shit back and, you know, and he knew that if, if he called the police then, you know, he ain't supposed to have none of that shit anyway because of the, the, the, the settlement that's against him, you know, the, you know, the money that he's supposed to be paying the Goldmans and shit so it's like if he called you guys he ain't gonna get the shit, the shit's going to be put into fucking, you know, and, you know, he's not going to get it. So I mean, he got this way, you know, he, you know, just like he does the signings and shit, you know, he's been making money but he does, he gets everything done under the table."

The shift from pointing toward McClinton's guilt to pointing to Simpson's greed hit a high point as Alexander explained:

"I just really haven't been, been, you know, having much to do with him (Simpson), you know, um, especially after he did the book, after I heard he wrote the book ("If I Did

It"), you know, I just felt like he was a piece of shit, you know, cause I mean I've been there, I know his kids. I'm like, you know, how dare this motherfucker do that, and the kids, I was, I knew that he, you know, he gets like $30,000 in, in monthly pension, you know, it's not like he needs the fucking money. It's just like this shit, he didn't need that shit, and he done fucked up this man's whole wedding because of his greed."

After the robbery, there was a dinner at a restaurant in the Palms Resort for the wedding party. Alexander said he expected we were going to show up at the party and arrest them; he knew it was coming. It was at this dinner that Alexander described Simpson as laughing about what had happened during the robbery and talking about Spencer being "a heavy-handed motherfucker." Simpson told them, "This is going to be all over the TV tomorrow, man. It's just gonna be everywhere." Alexander recalled Simpson telling them:

"Don't worry about it, you know, no guns were involved, you know, no guns was involved, long as there's no guns involved, you know, it ain't shit, just stick to no guns involved, you know, and uh, you know, I'm gonna tell 'em this and, you know, this is gonna go away. You know, don't worry about it, this will handle itself."

After listening to Simpson, Alexander asked, "If I go to jail, are you gonna bail me out?" Simpson told him not to worry about it, but Alexander never got an answer out of Simpson about bail. Alexander told McClinton, "That's a cheap motherfucker."

I didn't need much more from Alexander. He cleared up most of the details that didn't make sense and regardless of how much he avoided acknowledging that what they did was illegal, his statement was an indictment in itself. He was the first of the suspects who were arrested to confirm the details of what happened in Room 1203 and whether he knew it or not, he established they did, in fact, commit armed robbery, kidnapping with a firearm and burglary with a firearm and that there was a conspiracy involved for each one of those crimes. After we were done with the interview, Alexander also provided us with the local addresses of McClinton and Stewart.

It was a little after 4 p.m., and it was bound to be out soon that I had arrested Alexander. If I wanted to arrest the other suspects tonight, I needed to get moving. I still needed to get a search warrant for Alexander's luggage and get Alexander booked at Clark County Detention Center. Even though there was a deal in the works, Alexander still had to be charged with the crimes he committed and go through the court process, in which he would still have to plead guilty to a judge and have the judge agree with the sentence. Alexander eventually pleaded guilty to a felony conspiracy to commit robbery and for his cooperation, was sentenced to three years of probation.

With the assistance of Det. Bud Wolfenbarger, I obtained the search warrant for Alexander's luggage. I recovered Beardsley's stolen sunglasses and seized the clothing Alexander wore during the robbery.

# CHAPTER 7
# SEARCH WARRANTS

The information Alexander provided opened up new investigative leads that needed to be followed up on as soon as possible to avoid evidence being destroyed. It is the need to quickly move forward on new leads that can cause problems in the personal lives of police officers. Police departments are like many other businesses; there are hardworking and aggressive officers and there are officers who do just enough to get by. Between the personal drive within the more hardworking officers and the filtering system of selecting the best-qualified individuals for the more high-profile positions in a police department, you will often find the detectives who are selected to investigate crimes such as robbery and homicide are the officers who will sacrifice their personal lives to get the job done to the best of their ability. It is not uncommon to find detectives in robbery or homicide units to be working on their anniversaries, spouse's birthday, kids' birthdays and on holidays.

In 2006, I was investigating a robbery in which the suspect poured gasoline on my victim. When the victim would not give the suspect everything he wanted, the suspect lit a match and threw it on the victim. The victim died two days later. The crime caught the attention of local media and due to the victim being from Thailand; there was also a considerable amount of attention from the Thai Consulate. In the middle of following up on leads and identifying the suspect, I completely forgot my anniversary. I had sympathy from co-workers who had done the same thing in the past, but to me, that was not okay; I committed to myself and to my family to do a better job of balancing the demands of being a robbery detective with the need to be a good husband and father.

O.J. Simpson committed this crime in the evening on Thursday, Sept. 13. My regular days off at the time were Sundays, Mondays and Tuesdays. The leads Alexander gave me happened late in the afternoon on Saturday the 15th. Most of the time, I didn't mind working on my days off. But there were special occasions that if I were to work, it wouldn't just ruin my plans, it would ruin the plans of others, too. At the time of O.J.'s robbery in Las Vegas, my wife and I were youth leaders at our community church in Overton. For months, we had been planning a church youth trip to Dodger Stadium to see a game. The tickets already were bought and we had just enough drivers and cars to carpool everyone from our little rural community church to the game. It was an afternoon game on Sept. 16, and the plan was to drive down and back on the same day. It was important for me to go with my family and to not flake out on my commitment to my church.

It was about 8 p.m. when I got all the paperwork completed on the search warrant for Alexander's luggage and the evidence impounded. While I was working on that, Scott and Mark were working on verifying home addresses for Spencer/McClinton and Stewart, which Alexander had provided. Scott and Mark were able to obtain driver's license photos of the occupants of both residences. The picture of the occupant at the house where Alexander said Spencer lived was of McClinton, which Alexander confirmed as the man he knew as Spencer. Similarly, the house where Alexander said his friend C.J. lived ended up having an occupant named Clarence Stewart. Alexander looked at Stewart's driver's license picture and confirmed he was the man he knew as C.J. The driver's license pictures also matched the subjects in the surveillance video from the Palace Station of the suspects with O.J. Simpson.

I told Rod that I needed to leave by 8 a.m. "There is still a lot of work to be done tonight," Rod said, "but if you can get the search warrants done on McClinton's and Stewart's houses, then I don't see a problem with it." I had about 12 hours to get all of our new investigative leads wrapped up.

The search warrants I obtained for Room 1203 at the Palace Station and for Alexander's luggage were telephonic search warrants. My view of telephonic search warrants is that they are fast and sloppy and most effective when there is a minimal invasion on a person's Fourth Amendment rights against unreasonable search and seizure. The intrusion of a hotel room where nothing is sought to be seized other than forensic evidence and no damage is anticipated to the room is what I would consider a minimal invasion of a person's rights. The same can be said for the search of a piece of unlocked luggage that is already in the custody of law enforcement, where a reasonable argument could be made for safety reasons that the luggage needed to be searched anyway. Alexander was being arrested and his luggage either had to go to jail with him or I was going to have to impound it and neither was it safe nor allowable to take any personal property to the jail or impound any property that might have a gun or any other weapon inside. But a house is different. A non-consensual search of a person's residence is a significant invasion of that person's Fourth Amendment rights and it is not something to be done flippantly. For this reason, I felt it was best to obtain a search warrant in person from a judge.

Eddie started working on getting ownership records for the houses McClinton and Stewart were living in. Eddie also started working on identifying any other possible occupants who might be in the houses. Scott and Mark drove out to the two houses to get a description of the residences for a portion of the search warrant called the premise description, which is one of the requirements in a search warrant application. The premise description protects citizens from having their house searched by a mistake of transposing address numbers or going to Jones Avenue instead of Jones Road. A detailed premise description in a search warrant application offers an added level of protection for citizens against mistakes resulting in the wrong house getting searched. An example of a premise description would look something like this:

230 N. Moapa Valley Blvd. is a brown in color one story single family residence. It is located on the east side of Moapa Valley Blvd. north of Jones St. The front door to the residence is located on a room attached to the south side of the house, the front door is glass and faces west. The driveway for the house is asphalt and is located on the south side of the house. There is a chain-link fenced grass yard on the west side of the residence with a metal flagpole in the center of the grass area. Black numbers "230" are affixed to the eave above the front door.

Another key element required in the search warrant application is the probable cause, which describes the crime being investigated and what facts and circumstances have led the investigator to believe the location to be searched is connected to the crime being investigated. The last key element is to describe what the investigator is searching for. Police cannot get a search warrant to search for vague items such as illegal drugs. The application for a search warrant must be specific in listing the evidence sought to be seized such as methamphetamine or heroin. In this case, I was looking for the black handguns used during the robbery, memorabilia stolen during the robbery, clothing worn by the suspects during the robbery and items in each of the residences to establish a connection of each suspect to the house they live in. The items to connect the suspect to the residence they live in are oftentimes mail with the suspect's name and address, notes with names, pictures and similar type items.

Scott and Mark took pictures of both residences from their vehicle as they drove by to ensure I had a good premise description. When they showed me the pictures, I was caught off guard with how nice the houses were. I had envisioned smaller, single-story homes in lower-end neighborhoods.

That was not the case at all. Even though the suspects in the surveillance video appeared to me to be wannabe gangsters, their homes looked upper middle class and nicer than most homes in Las Vegas.

As I was finishing up typing the application for the search warrant, there were a few other important things going on in the background. It was getting late on a Saturday evening and I would need to find a judge who was home and able to review the search warrant application. If a detective is applying for a search warrant on Monday through Friday during business hours, you just simply go to the court and there are random signing judges who handle search warrant applications. The signing judges change from week to week, so you never know who you are going to get. Most detectives have an after-hours list of judges provided by the courts that contains judges' phone numbers and home addresses. Normally, I would first have to call an on-call deputy district attorney to get approval to apply for a search warrant, but for this search warrant, I already had the approval of the district attorney, so all that need to be done was finding an available judge. Eddie started working on finding a judge. "Judge shopping" is prohibited by our department policy; that is an unspoken process of only going to a judge you know is police friendly. Most detectives I know would never want to be involved in an unrighteous search warrant, so "judge shopping" was never an issue for me or anyone I worked around. There is no escaping the fact that some judges are rude jerks, which makes working with them difficult. A few judges make you feel like you were inconveniencing them by asking them to work when they were at home. Some would always be too busy when you asked if they were available to review a search warrant. And some would set unrealistic expectations such as giving you a small window of time to arrive at their house by. I never had a search warrant request denied, but I have been treated rudely by a few judges. Not calling certain judges who have treated me badly in the past to review a search warrant request was not "judge shopping," it was simply not creating an environment for a jerk to treat me like a jerk. I feel it is safe to say that Eddie shared my opinion about not calling judges who acted like detectives who were doing their jobs were an inconvenience and had the habit of treating us poorly. As I was getting close to finishing the application for the search warrants of McClinton and Stewart's residences, Eddie spoke with Judge Tony Abbatangelo, who was agreeable to allowing us to come to his home to review the request.

The other activity going on while I was finishing up on the request for the search warrant was the preparation work for the service of two search warrants. Serving search warrants on the residences of suspects involved in a violent crime with firearms requires specialized training, which most officers and detectives do not have. The LVMPD's SWAT section is the only unit allowed by our department to serve warrants like this. Serving two search warrants at two locations required almost the entire SWAT section to be called out on a Saturday night. Rod and Linda headed up getting the logistics in order to serve the warrants. It was not just SWAT that we would need; we also needed crime scene analysts and enough detectives at both locations to complete thorough searches. Both locations would need search warrant kits to include materials to recover and impound evidence and paperwork that is required to be completed before detectives leave the location of the search.

All of these actions need to be moving forward at the same time, which requires me as the lead detective to be using the detectives who I know are strong in managing administrative tasks. If I were to ask a junior detective with no experience to find and assign responsibilities for search teams at the residences, I would have had a nagging feeling that I needed to double check the work. Rod was making all the arrangements to work with the SWAT team. The same is true for an inexperienced sergeant. If I did not completely trust Rod and his ability to make all the arrangements to set up the briefings necessary to serve the search warrants, I would have felt I needed to double check everything to ensure the investigation did not suffer. Luckily, the robbery section was made up of some of the best detectives and supervisors on the LVMPD and with that knowledge, I could find peace in staying focused on getting the search warrants and knowing when I left the judge's house I could go straight over to a briefing, provide the teams with the information I needed them to know, and we could move forward with serving the search warrants.

After I finished typing, I gathered all the required paperwork so I would not have to come back to the office after I obtained the signed search warrants. Eddie and I headed over to Judge Abbatangelo's residence. It was almost midnight when we arrived. Most judges have big, beautiful homes and Judge Abbatangelo was no exception to that rule. He met us at the door and invited us in. The formality of court still exists even in the judge's home. He referred to us with our titles of "Detective" and we referred to him as "Judge" or "Your Honor." I handed the judge my application packet, which contained the application with the details of the probable cause and two search warrants for him to sign if he approved of the application. The actual search warrant is just three pages of paper containing the address to be searched, the items being searched for, the crime being investigated, any special orders from the judge, and the judge's signature block authorizing the search. Judge Abbatangelo took the packet and invited us to follow him to his dining room table. As he sat down, he invited us to sit while he reviewed my request. Eddie and I both chose to stand; for me, it feels weird to sit as equals with a judge under these types of circumstances. I believe we are all equal, but different positions demand a higher level of respect; positionally, I recognize a need to show this judge a level of respect that makes it clear I do not see myself as his peer. It took him about 20 minutes to review my application. Without much conversation, he pulled out the two search warrants and signed both, authorizing the search of McClinton's and Stewart's homes. Judge Abbatangelo handed me back the application with both signed search warrants on the top of the packet. He walked us to the door and said, "Good luck, gentlemen." At about 12:30 a.m. on Sunday, Eddie called Rod to tell him we had the search warrants in hand and they were signed. Rod knew everything about the case and got the briefings started so by the time Eddie and I got to the briefing location, all I needed to do was find out who was going to which location and make sure someone was assigned at both addresses to complete paperwork after each search warrant was served. I requested Eddie to take the lead of the search at McClinton's residence and Linda to take the lead of the search at Stewart's. Before we left, Rod told me he had established surveillance teams on both residences earlier in the evening and there had been no signs of occupants coming or going. Within a few minutes, the two SWAT teams loaded up into the tactical vehicles and headed over to the two search locations. It is an impressive sight: an armored truck followed by an SUV with special hand rails and foot stands on the outside of both sides, where men dressed in dark green tactical gear and armed with a variety of weapons stand and hold on. When they arrive, they are like a finely tuned machine; the SUV doesn't even come to a complete stop before the detectives dismount and fall into a formation to rapidly approach the target location behind the cover of the armored vehicle. Their movements are fast and smooth. They have the ability to be inside a violent offender's residence within seconds of arriving if they need to. Watching SWAT detectives conduct their duties is a great source of pride in our department for me. It amazes me to see the added risk these detectives take to keep our community safe.

As much as I enjoy watching SWAT teams serve search

warrants, I was not able to watch because I just didn't have the time. I needed to have Rod update me on anything I missed while I was working on the search warrant for Alexander's luggage and writing up the request for these two search warrants. We only had about 15 minutes of down time before we would need to be at McClinton's and Stewart's residences. Rod laughed and said, "You're not going to believe this, but I got a call from a parole officer out of California and he wanted me to arrest Alfred Beardsley." I was caught off guard and I didn't know what to say. Rod was told Beardsley was a "high control" parolee and not allowed to leave the state of California. Beardsley did a couple national media interviews and his parole officer saw him in Las Vegas, which was a violation of his parole conditions, so he needed to be arrested. It was late and we were in a parking lot standing outside of our vehicles. All I could do was shake my head and laugh. I had another six to eight hours of work ahead of me, so I figured the best way to look at Beardsley's situation was to acknowledge that I would at least know how to get hold of him if I needed him. Rod told the parole officer we were not going to arrest one of our victims, so he referred the parole officer to a unit in our department that would arrest Beardsley for them. I knew I would have to deal with that later, but we had to get going. The parking lot we were standing in was only a few blocks away from McClinton's house. Before we had the chance to get into our vehicles, the distinct sound of SWAT's distraction devices could be heard exploding and rocking the neighborhood. We knew that meant SWAT would be done shortly and we needed to get to the search locations.

I pulled into McClinton's neighborhood just as SWAT was advising that it was all clear for us to come up to the residence. The same thing was happening at Stewart's house at the same time only a few miles away. As I walked up to the residence, I was met by one of the SWAT detectives who told me the residence had been cleared and there was no one in the house. He showed me the damage to the front door that occurred when they made their entry and damage to a bedroom door upstairs that had been locked. After that, the SWAT guys loaded up in their armored truck and drove off, leaving behind the smell of gunpowder from the exploding distraction devices they used at the house.

Before we start to search, pictures are taken to document the condition of the house. Eddie took the lead on the search and assigned detectives to areas of the house. I had the living room and kitchen area, which was downstairs. Eddie and the other detectives went upstairs to search the bedroom and bathrooms. Administratively, I needed to find items to make sure this was McClinton's home. The evidence was overwhelming and indisputable; we found pictures, recent utility bills and documents with recent dates and his name. There was no doubt this was McClinton's home.

The search process is not a pretty one. We dump out drawers and remove them from cabinets. We remove clothes from closets and turn beds upside down. We empty out pantries and cupboards. Our searches are thorough because most detectives have experienced suspects hiding evidence and proceeds from crimes in places no normal, law-abiding citizen would even know existed in their own homes. I have found drugs in the ductwork of air conditioners and vents above the stove. I have found a gun taped inside a washing machine where the bottom panel had to be removed to access it. I have found a bag of a precursor to make methamphetamine inside an empty metal box inside a working computer. Some suspects hide evidence in crazy places, so we have to search everything. We might leave a mess, but we rarely damage anything.

As I am finishing up with the kitchen, Eddie called me upstairs. In dresser drawers in the master bedroom, they had located two black handguns that were exactly as Alexander had described.

I seized the two handguns: a black .22 caliber Beretta

and .45 caliber Ruger. Also located in McClinton's bedroom was a concealed weapons permit for the handguns that were found and a suit that appeared to be what he wore during the armed robbery. I was excited about finding the guns, even though we had yet to find any of the stolen memorabilia.

The search was wrapping up at McClinton's residence and I needed to go over to Stewart's house. Eddie was taking care of the paperwork at this location, so I left to go over to the other search. When I arrived at Stewart's house, the detectives there were also just finishing up. Linda briefed me on their search. They found the large plaid shirt Stewart was wearing during the armed robbery, but they did not find any of the memorabilia, either. It was about 5 a.m. when we all got back to the office. We worked together to impound the evidence from the search warrants and complete the paperwork so we could secure for the day. I, again, had been at work for more than 20 hours and knew I still had a long day ahead of me. As we were leaving that Sunday morning, Eddie and I agreed we would come in on Monday morning and pick up where we left off. I would renew my application for an arrest warrant of O.J. Simpson with the new evidence of the last two days.

# CHAPTER 8
# O.J.'S ARREST

There have been very few times in my career that I have been truly disappointed with my co-workers. The actions of a few detectives on Sept. 16, 2007, were one of those disheartening times. Eddie and I only had about 12 hours off from work since the robbery had happened on the evening of Sept. 13, and now on the morning of the 16th, we were going to get some time off.

I did not have time to take the hour-long drive home to the community where I live because I was going to Los Angeles that afternoon for the Dodgers game. My plan was to sleep on the way to L.A. while my wife drove. Then I could watch the game with my family and church friends and drive back home that evening. By the time my wife picked me up, I had caught a quick nap in my car and, as we were leaving the office parking lot, the day shift robbery detectives who work on the days my squad didn't, were starting to filter in for the start of their workweek. As we headed toward the freeway, we joined up with the caravan of people from our church who were going with us.

The robbery section was made up of four squads. There were two day-shift squads and two swing-shift squads. The week was divided in half with Wednesday being the common day that all four squads worked together. Every other day of the week, there are just two squads working—one day shift and one swing shift. I worked on the swing-shift squad that had Sunday, Monday and Tuesday off. Scott and Mark worked on the day-shift squad with the same days off. Sept. 16, 2007, was a Sunday, so the day-shift squad that started work this morning had nothing to do with the armed robbery investigation involving O.J. Simpson.

I cannot emphasize this point enough: they had nothing

to do with my case.

There are certain personalities that seem to be drawn to police work. I don't want to overgeneralize here, but I know many officers who have aggressive and dominant personalities. And most officers I know who are in the more elite units of the LVMPD are naturally competitive. Even with that, there are some unspoken rules that I feel are universal. While I might not be able to defend a bad decision of another officer or detective, I will always protect their safety; that is universal.

New Year's Eve in Las Vegas is an interesting celebration. Hundreds of thousands of tourists flock to the Strip to celebrate the ushering in of a new year. This presents a precarious situation for police officers to ensure tourists' safety when the crowds get so thick that people cannot move around without having to push through a crowd in all directions. The police officers stand in a safe zone behind barriers and monitor the crowds. It is a dangerous environment for officers to go into the crowd when it is so thick that no one is moving. Even though it is dangerous, there are times when officers must go in to protect others. On the New Year's Eve of 1999 to 2000, the Las Vegas Strip was especially crowded. Without any warning or planning, one of the officers on the squad I was working on jumped over the barrier into the crowd. There were people in the crowd who had just been in a fight and words were still being exchanged by the two groups; it was a volatile environment and there was a high probability of the officer getting hurt by going into the crowd alone. No matter what his intentions were, there was an automatic response of half our squad jumping the barriers and going into the crowd to bring him out safely.

Another universal rule is that you never take credit for another detective's work and you don't meddle in cases you have nothing to do with. This one is big and I believe there are only certain types of people who engage in this behavior. In 2006, there was a subject who had escaped from a Nevada

State Prison, where he was serving a prison sentence for armed robbery. After he escaped, he came back to Las Vegas and started committing the exact types of crimes he went to prison for. Detectives labeled this subject "The Cancer Bandit" before he was caught and sent to prison. He would go into a business and rob the employees and patrons at gunpoint, telling them he never would commit that type of crime normally, but his son had cancer and he needed money so he could save his son's life. There was no truth to the story, but oftentimes, it worked on victims who would then feel bad for the guy who had just taken their purses and wallets at gunpoint. Though the victims would call the police to report their property stolen, some would not want to report the robbery because they did not want to see him get into trouble. Det. Eric Stout was the lead detective on the robbery cases that happened after the subject escaped from prison. One night after another robbery, we were close to catching the suspect, but after a series of home invasions and car jackings, the suspect got away. The case was aired on "America's Most Wanted" and within a day, a tip came in to report where the suspect was hiding. After another home invasion in which the suspect took an elderly couple hostage, LVMPD's SWAT detectives were able to successfully take the subject into custody without the hostages being harmed. After the suspect was sent back to prison, officers and detectives were nominated for an award for their involvement in the investigation and re-apprehension of the suspect. The interesting thing was there were detectives who received the award who did nothing award-worthy; they might have shown up at a crime scene or had their name on a report, but they had no real responsibility or assumed risk. Nonetheless, they received the award. When it comes down to receiving accolades for another person or other people's work, there are some individuals who lack the intestinal fortitude to admit they don't deserve recognition for other people's work.

This same principle applies to individuals who would use other people's work to gain glory for themselves. It is something cops should not do to other cops. But it happens.

I was sleeping on the way to Los Angeles in a van full of teenagers. When we were about 30 minutes away from Dodger Stadium, I was woken up by my phone ringing. My caller ID showed it was Det. Laura Anderson from the LVMPD homicide section. Before Laura went to the homicide section, she and I were on the same robbery squad. I figured she was calling to ask questions about the Simpson armed robbery, so I answered the phone. "Congratulations," she said instantly. It took me a moment to shake all the sleep out of my mind and I really did not know what she meant. "Congratulations on what?" She was genuinely happy and said, "For arresting O.J." I told her I had not arrested him yet and that I had only submitted for an arrest warrant that was not approved yet. She said the local news stations had got their facts mixed up and were reporting he had been arrested. I told her I had only left the office a few hours ago and I could definitely say O.J. had not been arrested. We were close enough to the stadium that I was not going back to sleep. Even after I got off the phone, I still chuckled at how bad the news can mess up a story. About 10 minutes later, my phone rings again. It's Laura calling again, so I answer, figuring she is going to tell me how she misunderstood the news report. I could not have been more wrong. Laura explained to me that I needed to call my office to find out what is going on because the news is reporting specifics about O.J. being arrested that same morning at the Palms Resort and Casino. I was definitely caught off guard, because Laura seemed convinced the news reports were accurate. I know my partners well enough to know they would have called me if there were a new development. This did not make sense.

I called Eddie and after multiple rings, he answered the phone. He clearly had been sleeping. I asked him if he had heard anything about Simpson being arrested at the Palms.

Eddie was caught off guard as much as I was. I asked Eddie to call the office to see what was going on.

As I waited for Eddie to call me back, I asked my wife to turn the car radio to sports radio to see if there was any news being reported about Simpson being arrested. After a few minutes passed, I had not heard anything on the news. Eddie called me back.

The day-shift robbery squad that had nothing to do with any aspect of the investigation went out, arrested Simpson and transported him back to the robbery office.

There is no doubt they had approval from someone in our chain of command to make the arrest, but there is only a handful of detectives or officers who would actually go out and make an arrest like this without the common courtesy of reaching out to those who had done the work to let them know what they were doing. I will even take that a step farther and say that most detectives and police officers would refuse to go out and make an arrest like this without contacting the detectives who had done the work. They did not even take the minute it would have taken to call Eddie or me to let us know what was going on.

This was a clear case of a group of individuals ignoring what they knew was the right thing to do because their eyes were fixed on getting to say they arrested O.J. Simpson. There cannot even be an argument made of some sense of urgency to justify their actions. Even if there were reasonable information received that Simpson was leaving Las Vegas that day, Eddie, Linda and Rod could have been called out and been at the Palms Resort just as fast as the squad of detectives who had nothing to do with the case. It is common for robbery detectives to be called out from home on their off time to handle cases. But if that squad had called even one of the detectives involved in the case, they would not have gotten to tell everyone they arrested O.J. Simpson.

There are only two ways to arrest a person. Either an officer has an arrest warrant signed by a judge or the officer has sufficient probable cause to make the arrest. There was not an arrest warrant issued for Simpson, so his arrest required probable cause, which exists when the facts and circumstances known to the officer would warrant a prudent person in believing that a crime had been committed and that the accused had committed it. So even if there were someone in the chain of command who was now saying the LVMPD robbery section could make the arrest of O.J. Simpson, there was only a handful of individuals who knew the facts and circumstances of the crimes and that Simpson had committed them. Make no mistake—if this were not O.J. Simpson, these detectives would have never risked arresting someone without an arrest warrant or without the detectives who knew the facts and circumstances of the case. Eddie headed to the robbery office where the other squad had transported Simpson. The rest of our robbery squad met Eddie there. The other squad had to bring Simpson to the office because they did not have the ability to book him; none of them could write an arrest report because they had no knowledge of the case. This points to the simple fact they knew they were going to have to call in the detectives who actually worked the investigation, but they weren't going to do it until after they got their moment of glory.

Eddie now had to put together an arrest packet. Most of the packet was already done and just had to be reprinted from the request for an arrest warrant I had submitted on the morning after the armed robbery at the Palace Station. There was more evidence to add at this point, so Eddie needed to combine the affidavit requesting the arrest warrant from the 14th with arrest report for Walter Alexander's arrest on the 15th. Between these reports, Eddie completed an arrest report on Orenthal James Simpson and he was transported to Clark County Detention Center, where he was booked for his involvement in the armed robbery on Sept. 13, 2007.

Eddie kept me posted by phone of what he was doing. One of Eddie's phone calls was very angry. "You're not going to believe this. He filled out a TCR and he signed his name as the arresting officer." For every person arrested and taken to jail, law enforcement must complete a Temporary Custody Report (TCR), which contains the suspect's personal information, the charges the suspect is being arrested for and who the arresting officer is. One of the detectives from the squad that went out and arrested Simpson without any knowledge of the case had come back and filled out one piece of paper listing himself as the arresting officer. I asked Eddie what he did with it and he laughed, saying, "I ripped it up." Of the thousands of commissioned officers on the LVMPD, there are only a few who are so oblivious to common courtesy in police culture that would claim an arrest they had nothing to do with and one of those people just happened to be a robbery detective.

Eddie had already thrown the TCR in the trash, but I asked him to get it out and put it on my desk. I wanted to keep it as a reminder of the importance of ethical behavior—not just in my interactions with the public, but also with my co-workers. I taped it back together and I still have it as I'm writing this.

On Sept. 16, 2007, Simpson was arrested for two counts of robbery with a deadly weapon, two counts of assault with a deadly weapon, burglary with a deadly weapon and conspiracy to commit a crime. It is common for detectives to make an arrest and after the District Attorney's Office reviews the facts and circumstances of the crime, prosecutors can amend the charges based on what they can prove. In this case, the DA's Office added the charges of two counts of kidnapping with a deadly weapon, conspiracy to commit kidnapping, conspiracy to commit burglary and two counts of coercion with a deadly weapon.

Even though I set out with the goal of going to a baseball game and not letting my work affect my time with my family, the reality was that it did. I did get to watch the game, but my mind was divided between the game and what was going on in Vegas. My wife had made the arrangements for the bulk ticket purchase for the game and when she did, they offered to welcome our little country church on the stadium big screen display during the game. When I saw "Welcome Calvary Community Church" on the display board, it was a great moment to just forget about O.J. Simpson. It was great to see how excited people from our church got to see that short message and it was a nice reminder for me of the importance of time with family and friends no matter how busy life gets. Up until that moment, I was not sure I had made the right decision to go to the game rather than stay in Vegas, but I can look back and safely say my kids and the kids from our church have great memories from that Dodgers game and I would not want to have missed that for the world.

After the game was over, I got a call from Eddie. They were done for the day and headed back home. Even though Simpson was in custody, I knew there was still a mountain of work to do when I got back. As we drove into Las Vegas later that evening, my wife dropped me off so I could pick up my car and she followed me home to make sure I didn't fall asleep at the wheel.

On Monday, Sept. 17, I came into the office early in the morning to get a head start on the day and arrived before the detectives from the other squad came in. I needed to make copies of some paperwork for the case file, so I went into the copy room. Before I started copying, I checked the printer tray where the copies come out because inevitably, someone will have printed something from their desk and will have forgotten to get it off the printer. Sure enough, there were some papers in the tray. I picked up a stack of about 10 papers and walked back out into the bay where all the detective's desks were, intending to put the printed documents on the desks of those who had printed them. As I flipped through the pages, there were four full-sized pictures that had clearly been left on the printer by mistake. It was only two pictures and each one was printed twice. Each picture was from the surveillance camera in the robbery/homicide interview rooms with two of the detectives from the squad who had decided to go arrest Simpson without telling the detectives who had done the work. These two detectives took turns going into the interview room and pretended to be interviewing Simpson while the other one went and pushed a button to take a still picture from the surveillance video system. They clearly took turns doing this to allow for each one to have a picture with Simpson in the interview room. I placed the pictures on the center of each one of their desks so they would know the pictures had been found. I had too much work to do to sit and dwell on their behavior, so I chalked it up to the personification of how the less than 1 percent of police officers engage in behavior that can give the rest of us a bad rap.

# CHAPTER 9
# MEMORABILIA

Sept. 17, 2007, was a day full of curveballs for the investigation. Rod had received a call from a local defense attorney named Robert Lucherini saying he represented Stewart, who wanted to turn himself in at 2:30 p.m. at Lucherini's office. The news of Simpson's arrest prompted some of the other suspects to want to turn themselves in.

Outside of dealing directly with the suspects, I had a few other loose ends that needed to be tied up. Fromong was on the phone with a lady he identified as Christie Lutkemeier when the suspects entered the room. I wanted to talk with Lutkemeier to learn if she heard anything that would be of value to the investigation and me. I called the number Fromong gave me for Lutkemeier, but there was no answer, so I left a message. Within a few minutes, I received a call from a man identifying himself as an attorney named Ken Miller representing Lutkemeier, who did not want to make a statement unless the District Attorney's Office gave her immunity from prosecution. There are some people who are simply addicted to attention and a desire to make themselves more important than they are and I got the distinct impression that I was dealing with one of those people. I politely explained how I was looking to know if she had heard anything before Fromong hung up the phone the night he was robbed. He insisted on immunity. It was clear to me she was going to try to muddy up the investigation with irrelevant nonsense and I had no time for that; I tried to let her tell me what she heard, but she wanted special treatment.

Within an hour of getting off the phone with Lutkemeier's attorney, I received a call from another attorney who identified himself as John Howes from Florida. Howes told me he represented one of the unidentified male suspects from the armed robbery who wanted to turn himself in without being arrested. He refused to give me the name of the suspect he represented and all I could think was, "Why is this guy even calling me?" I think this attorney thought I was going to stop everything I was doing and work on making his client avoid jail for the crime his client committed. Our criminal justice system can seem a little off when defense attorneys make criminals out to be victims and police officers out to be criminals. At the time of this call, I was not even a little concerned about not being able to identify the outstanding suspects, so there was nothing of value this attorney could offer me at this time. I could care less if his client came back to turn himself in or if I obtained an arrest warrant and had him brought back to Nevada against his will. Either way, it was only a matter of time before he went to jail. As I hung up, I had a moment to think about how our conversation probably didn't go as well as he expected.

Within an hour, another attorney named Linda Norvell called the robbery office trying to reach me, but I was unable to take the call. She left a message saying she was calling on McClinton's behalf because he now wanted to turn himself in as well. Norvell was a local attorney who went to law school with a friend of mine, so as a courtesy to my friend, I called her back as soon as I got the message, but she was out for lunch. Subjectivity is another uncomfortable truth about my experience with the criminal justice system. I would love to walk away after 20 plus years of working in law enforcement and say the system is completely objective, but it's not. There is an observable good ol' boy system with judges and attorneys. One attorney can walk into a courtroom late and the judge will make the attorney wait. A more popular attorney can walk into the same courtroom late and the judge will put that case on top of the stack to be heard. I believe this is a relational issue and it is unavoidable; some people like each other and some don't. On the rare occasion, it does have a negative impact on victims.

My partner was working on a complex fraud and theft investigation that spanned over the course of three years. It involved corrupt public officials, attorneys, police officers and construction companies. During one of the scams pulled on a group of victims, more than $200,000 was stolen out of an account. Shortly after the money was stolen, one of the main suspects retained one of the most high-profile and well-liked attorneys in Las Vegas for the same amount of money that was stolen out of the account. The money seemed to be proceeds from criminal activity and it was brought to the attention of the prosecutor handling the case. Unfortunately, the prosecutor did not want to see the possibility that this well-liked attorney could have taken stolen money and was not interested in exploring ways to recover the victims' money that the suspect had stolen. The defense attorney was allowed to keep what I believed was stolen money as his retainer and represented the suspect against the fraud charges. The suspect went to prison, the victims did not get restitution and the defense attorney kept the money. This case was extreme and it is rare to see that level of "professional courtesy" among lawyers, but it does happen and it sucks.

Sometimes, the subjective nature of the officials in the criminal justice system can work in the victim's favor, too. There can be certain crimes that judges are harder on than others, according to their personal set of principles.

In the Moapa Valley Justice Court in Clark County, Judge Lanny Waite receives many pleas to many different crimes. The vast majority of times I have been in the courtroom, Judge Waite accepts the terms of the plea bargain arranged between the prosecutor and defense attorney. One of the sweeter moments as a police officer is when a suspect you arrested gets offered and accepts a plea bargain that does not seem fair for the gravity of crime that was committed, then after the suspect enters a plea of guilty, the judge changes the punishment. As a suspect enters into an agreement with the prosecutor and defense attorney, the suspect is told the judge does not have to agree to the terms submitted, even though most times judges do keep the terms that are agreed upon. Before a suspect finds out if the judge is going to agree with the terms of the plea agreement, the suspect must first admit guilt and cannot retract it. With Judge Waite, when the plea agreement offered is too light, he changes the agreed-upon punishment and adds additional stipulations to the sentence. Sometimes it is a little more than a fine and other times and can be more time in jail. Even when this happens, it still seems like the suspect is getting off too easy, but most police officers find joy in those small justices.

I was fielding more phone calls from attorneys in one afternoon than I normally would get in a year. I received another message to call an attorney named Jonathan Palak, who represented the Goldman family in the civil settlement against Simpson for the 1994 death of Ron Goldman. Palak was curious if we had recovered any of the property stolen from the hotel room to see if there was anything of value that might have actually belonged to Simpson and should be turned over to the Goldmans pursuant to the court order in California against Simpson. At this point, I had only recovered Beardsley's sunglasses that were stolen, so I was not able to help Palak in that matter.

Simpson's defense was telling anyone who would listen that he was just taking his own property back—that the stuff taken from the room was property that belonged to Simpson. This was simply a narrative created to make Simpson's actions not look so bad in the court of popular opinion. As I listened to Palak, I picked up on some interesting things. Simpson cannot own valuable memorabilia and if he did own any, it would be ordered seized by the courts and sold to go toward the money he owes the Goldmans. I asked Palak for the court paperwork that explains what items of value Simpson must turn over. Palak referred me to an attorney named David Cook, who dealt specifically with collecting Simpson's debt to the Goldmans. Cook provided me with court-ordered interrogatories from Simpson about property of value he owns. An interrogatory is a fancy way of describing a written questionnaire that must be answered as a result of a court action. I saw value in the interrogatories if the need arose to dispute the claim that Simpson was just taking his own property back. In the paperwork Cook provided me, there was no evidence of Simpson claiming he owned any of the property Fromong had reported as stolen. This was not a big worry because he stole Joe Montana and West Point memorabilia, too, but it is always a good idea to have more evidence than is needed to prove a case.

Palak and Cook were both very helpful in explaining the logistics of Simpson's outstanding debt that he is legally bound to pay and how he had worked loopholes to avoid paying the money he owed. They were aware of his unreported income through the memorabilia underworld. However, there was no way to know when he was getting money or how much. I think it was during my conversations with Palak and Cook that it hit me how some segments of our twisted culture can help facilitate someone like Simpson to still live like a star. I guess I would not have minded too much if he were paying on his debt for the offense he was found guilty of in a civil court; but the fact he was not even making attempts made me frustrated at the sycophants who buy his memorabilia because it helps to support his extravagant lifestyle. There is some strange irony in the thought that Simpson will point to his acquittal for the murders of Nicole Brown and Ron Goldman as proof of his innocence; in this case, he wants others to accept the court's decision. Yet in the court's decision in 1997, a civil jury unanimously found Simpson accountable for the wrongful deaths of Ron Goldman and Nicole Brown, and he was ordered to pay $33.5 million in damages. He does not put effort into accepting the verdict of the court's decision for him to pay millions in damages. Instead, he takes trips to Las Vegas, where he stays in an extravagant suite and enjoys celebrity treatment. The more information Cook and Palak provided me with, the more I saw Simpson as a greed-driven narcissist.

My day of dealing with attorneys was not over yet. I still needed to go to Lucherini's office to arrest Stewart. Lucherini's office was in downtown Las Vegas just a mile or so away from Fremont Street, where most the tourists who frequent downtown go to enjoy the traditional Las Vegas casinos. There was a residential area in downtown Las Vegas from the 1960s that had been converted to commercial use. These houses that were converted to businesses were on streets with large mature trees that provide abundant shade from the desert heat. They have large, well-groomed grass yards, which are becoming more and more rare in the Las Vegas area. These older neighborhoods have law offices scattered throughout them. These neighborhoods seem out of place for being downtown. To the west, you will find both city and county government buildings surrounded with high-end condos. To the north, there is low-rent housing and old run-down apartments. To the south, there is a commercial area with gas stations and older businesses. To the east, there are gang-filled neighborhoods. In the middle of all that are these old converted homes that provide a warm and inviting atmosphere to anyone who drives through.

Just after 2:30 p.m., Eddie and I pulled up outside Lucherini's office. It was like most of the other offices, with a large tree providing shade for a sidewalk that led right to the entrance. As we crossed the street, I noticed a greenish Lincoln Navigator parked right in front of the office. I knew it was Stewart's based on records I had already completed on him. Eddie and I walked into a waiting room with a receptionist. I introduced myself and told her we were there for Clarence Stewart. She quickly told me that Mr. Lucherini was expecting us and asked us to wait a moment while she let him know we had arrived. I was expecting him to make us wait for a few minutes, but I was wrong. Before Eddie and I had a chance to sit down, Lucherini opened a door to the waiting room and introduced himself.

Over the years, I have come to believe that most defense attorneys are shifty and untrustworthy. They seem to always be working angles to use to benefit their clients later in court. I find that even in a setting like this, where I am just there to arrest his client, Lucherini being a defense attorney will still try to manipulate me and twist my words to use against me later during court proceedings. That might seem paranoid, but it is a safe thought process to have when dealing with defense attorneys.

Both Eddie and I towered over Lucherini. He was wearing a shirt and tie with his sleeves rolled up. Without giving us much opportunity to talk, he invited us into his office. I already didn't like how he seemed to be hurrying us and trying to control our short introduction by not even allowing Eddie and me to respond in kind to his introduction; he was pushy. He walked ahead of us and sat behind a desk so large it made him look even smaller than he was. Stewart sat in one of the chairs in front of Lucherini's desk.

Lucherini started off the conversation by telling us his client might be willing to give us a statement if there was some room to negotiate a deal. Under normal circumstances, that would have been a ridiculous request and I would have just said we had no authority to discuss deals with a defense attorney. He was trying to imply his client could explain to us everything that happened the night of the robbery. The problem with Lucherini wanting a deal for his client was that he didn't have information I needed. Alexander had already provided the details I needed to provide an investigative foundation to uncover the facts of the armed robbery. Lucherini made a point of telling us how he used to work at the DA's Office with Roger before he was elected as the district attorney. Lucherini asked if I could call Roger to learn if there could be any consideration given if Stewart made a statement about the night of the robbery.

I stepped outside and called Roger, explaining that I was

about to make another arrest in the case at Robert Lucherini's office. Lucherini was dropping Roger's name, asking for a deal for the suspect I was about to arrest. Roger laughed and said, "His client can make a statement if he would like, but as of now, he will be arrested for the crimes he committed." Roger asked me to serve Stewart with a notice of intent to seek indictment for the armed robbery. After a suspect has been served with a notice, the prosecutor can opt to have the case heard before a grand jury instead of the normal preliminary hearing process. As I told Lucherini what Roger had instructed, I could see he was disappointed. He glanced over to Stewart as if to provide Stewart some reassurance that everything is still going to be okay.

Lucherini's office was nice; it had bookshelves full of law books and conversation pieces. I was standing in front of Lucherini's desk just off to his left and Stewart was sitting in a chair to my left. Eddie was walking around the office looking at the various keepsakes on the bookshelves. He had old model trains and cars, and magnetically powered moving trinkets. As I was in mid-sentence, I heard Eddie angrily growl, "Are you fuckin' recording us?" I looked back toward Eddie, who was standing by a tall bookcase in the back of the office. Before I had a chance to say anything, Eddie continued and he was clearly getting angrier as every second ticked by. "What is this shit? You're fuckin' recording us and you don't even have the professional courtesy to tell us? That's bullshit!" Eddie reached behind some books on the bookshelf where he saw the red glow from a light on a micro-recorder Lucherini had hidden and turned on before we entered the room. Eddie brought the recorder over to Lucherini and told him, "I don't give a shit if you record us. We're here as a courtesy to you and if I wanted to arrest your client right now, I would. We've extended the courtesy of taking the time to talk with you and you repay us with this bullshit." As Eddie handed the recorder to Lucherini, he turned off the recorder and said he was sorry. Eddie was right, Lucherini said, and it was inappropriate to record us without telling us. Legally, Lucherini did not commit a crime by recording us, but I think Eddie was so loud and visibly angry that he scared Lucherini and threw him off his game. The tone of our meeting completely changed after Eddie found the recorder. Lucherini seemed like a child who had gotten in trouble and was now trying to please his parents.

Lucherini told me he would like to provide a summary of his client's actions the evening of the armed robbery. Stewart sat quietly in his chair as Lucherini talked. Lucherini claimed Simpson had asked Stewart multiple times throughout the day to go with him and help him get his property back. At around 7 p.m. on the night of the armed robbery, Stewart was at a KFC restaurant with Scotto and Arnelle Simpson, O.J.'s daughter. Stewart drove Scotto and Arnelle to the Palms Resort and Casino. He claimed O.J. Simpson was there with two other guys Stewart did not know when Scotto and Arnelle got out of Stewart's vehicle. Stewart was directed to the Palace Station, where they met two guys in suits. Lucherini did not provide the name of the guys in the suits, but as this point, I knew them to be Alexander and McClinton. Lucherini provided the entry order of the suspects into the room for the armed robbery, identifying the first person in as Riccio. The next were the two males who I had not yet identified. He claimed it was Simpson next, then the two men in the suits. And, of course, Lucherini offered up that his client was the last one in the room and did not see anyone waving or pointing guns. Lucherini claimed that Stewart thinks the guys with the guns just kept them at their sides. Lucherini was clearly trying to make lemonade out of lemons by adding as much sugar to Stewart's story while still admitting some wrongdoing. He explained Stewart did a "pat down" of the victims to look for guns. He claimed the victims were telling Simpson and the other suspects to just take the property and that the victims even helped to pack up the property. During the armed robbery, the victims did say some of the items did not belong to Simpson, to which Simpson responded that he would return the items that were not his. After the armed robbery, Stewart drove Simpson back to the Palms, where he claimed Simpson got out of the vehicle and told Stewart to keep the property. Lucherini said the Montana lithographs and Fromong's cell phone were given to one of the guys who Stewart knew only as "Chuck."

Lucherini walked to a door in the back of his office by the bookshelf where Eddie found the recorder. He opened a door that led to a conference room with a large table. On the table were two white pillowcases that were obviously full of footballs, a cardboard box full of books, a couple of boxes containing 8x10 signed O.J. Simpson pictures and one box of larger 11x14 signed O.J. Simpson pictures, Beardsley's baseball hat, two framed plaques and one framed picture. Eddie called LVMPD dispatch and requested a crime scene analyst be dispatched to our location. We did not touch the items in the room and I requested that everyone stay out of the room until the evidence could be photographed and processed for fingerprints.

Within a short time, Crime Scene Analyst (CSA) A. Nemcik arrived. I was excited to see what was in the room; it was great to recover the victim's property, but I was also curious to see the footballs and plaques. CSA Nemcik pulled six footballs out of the first pillowcase: Simpson's Hall of Fame football, the 4 Touchdown football, the 273 Rushing Yard football, the signed 1975 Kodak All-Star football and two commemorative rushing yard footballs. The pillowcase also contained a yellow necktie, which is claimed to be one of the neckties Simpson wore during his 1995 trial. The second pillowcase contained five footballs: the 250 Rushing Yard football, another Hall of Fame football recording 10,183 Rushing Yards, the signed 1968 Kodak All-Star football, a commemorative Heisman Trophy football and a commemorative West Point football. The box of books contained 18 limited edition "I Want To Tell You" books by O.J. Simpson. There were 11 different types of signed O.J. Simpson pictures. The two plaques were Simpson's

All-America Award and a certificate marking his selection to the AFL All-Star Team. The framed picture was a signed photo of O.J. Simpson with J. Edgar Hoover. And lastly, when CSA Nemcik picked up Beardsley's hat, there were two more neckties inside, both claimed to have been worn during Simpson's 1995 trial.

I told Lucherini that I needed to serve Stewart with a notice of intent to seek indictment for the armed robbery. I filled out the form and handed it to Lucherini while Stewart was still sitting in the chair. Lucherini explained the notice to Stewart and then signed it for Stewart. Stewart was then arrested and booked into the Clark County Detention Center.

When I spoke with Roger while at Lucherini's office, he also asked me to serve O.J. Simpson with a notice of intent to seek indictment when I had a chance. While we were at the Clark County Detention Center, I requested Simpson be brought up to a private interview room so I could serve him with paperwork. Two corrections officers brought him to the interview room. He was wearing a blue jail jumpsuit and, when the corrections officer opened the door to the room where Eddie and I were waiting, Simpson got a big smile on his face and said, "Hi, guys." As if he was happy to see us. The form is simple and straightforward; it lists the crimes suspected and the date the crimes are suspected to have been committed. It also is addressed to the party being accused. Simpson read the document, but did not question it. I handed him my pen and told him I needed him to sign the form acknowledging he received it. He signed his signature next to the line that states, "I certify that I have received the above Notice of Intent to Seek Indictment." As I looked at his signature on this document, I had a moment to reflect on how many times he has signed his name on memorabilia for personal gain over the last few years. But the signature he just gave me marked the initiation of a legal process that would eventually send him to prison for the first time in his life.

# CHAPTER 10
## TMZ TAPES

After finishing the arrest and booking paperwork on Clarence Stewart and serving O.J. Simpson with his Notice of Intent to Seek Indictment at the Clark County Detention Center, Eddie and I drove back to the Robbery Office. It was a good day and we had been able to get a large amount of work done on the case. In the car, we had a moment to reflect on something District Attorney David Roger had told us when we arrested Walter Alexander; Roger had pulled Eddie and me aside before I interviewed Alexander and said, "Gentlemen, this is about to be the biggest case you will ever be involved in." Everything was happening so fast when he said that to us I don't think either of us had the time to fully appreciate what he had said. But now only four days later, Simpson was in custody along with two of his co-conspirators, most of the property had been recovered, and the three outstanding suspects were going to be easy to identify and get into custody. At this point I was able to confirm most of the property stolen by Simpson and his men did not and had never belonged to O.J. Simpson. The last few days had been mostly good and full of moments that I will never forget. That evening I had a tremendous sense of satisfaction and accomplishment on drive from the Clark County Detention Center to the Robbery Office.

My sense of accomplishment was bolstered by random contacts and phone calls I had with other officers and detectives around the police department. I was getting regular congratulations about "getting O.J." I'm sure those congratulations meant different things from different people, but no one was making a big deal about Stewart or Alexander being arrested for the same crime; the outside perspective was centered on O.J. Simpson being arrested. For as much as I focused on treating this armed robbery objectively, I would be lying to myself if I did not acknowledge that most of my sense of accomplishment revolved around Simpson's involvement and being able to put a solid case together against him. There is always a sense of satisfaction in catching a bad guy who hurt someone or had committed some crime, but this was different: it was O.J. Simpson. If this exact same robbery happened but Simpson was not involved, it would not have even caused a discussion beyond an initial briefing for supervisors because it happened in a casino. Other than that, Eddie and I would have run through our investigation, arrested suspects and recovered what property we could; it would have been no different than the 20 other robbery cases I received each month as a robbery detective. Another aspect of my feeling of satisfaction was rooted in my perception that nothing had gone wrong that would cause our department or us any embarrassment. And truth be told, I now had time to reflect how much overtime I worked over the last few days and how nice of a paycheck I was going to be receiving.

Linda was sitting at her desk when Eddie and I walked into our office. There were reports that needed to be updated and finished, but I was able to put that off for a few minutes. For the first time since I responded to the armed robbery call at the Palace Station, I had a chance to go online and read some news. I knew from family and friends how Simpson's armed robbery and arrest had consumed much of the news cycle and I had been told about Riccio and Beardsley giving interviews to anyone with a camera, but I did not get to experience the Simpson media blitz until this moment. As I began to read through some of the stories, I laughed at how many comments were being made about conspiracies and how the police were framing O.J. Simpson. After reading through a few stories, I heard Linda call out for Eddie and me to come over to her desk. Linda pointed to her computer and said, "I don't know what they have, but they claim they have a recording of the robbery." Linda was on a news page and there was a pop-up from TMZ claiming it had an audio recording of the armed robbery committed by O.J. Simpson in a Las Vegas hotel and casino. It was just a teaser that announced TMZ would not be releasing it until a certain time later that evening. As we waited for the release, I struggled to understand how there could be a recording of the robbery; that feeling of accomplishment because we had not embarrassed ourselves or our department was now feeling like it might be in jeopardy. My thoughts started to wander to a place of concern that this could've been some sort of setup beyond what I knew Riccio had done. All I could do was wait. Eddie and I stood at Linda's cubicle until the time came for TMZ to play what it had. TMZ played a six-minute audio recording of what was clearly the robbery at the Palace Station. At this point, I was familiar enough with the voices of the people I had contact with to recognize the voices of Riccio, Fromong, Beardsley, O.J. Simpson, Alexander and Stewart. The audio was poor quality, but from the first time I listened to the audio, it was apparent to me there was anger in the voice of Simpson and the men he brought with him, and there was fear in the voices of Fromong and Beardsley. It was an odd feeling of relief; I felt bad for what the victims had to go through, but I did not want a new revelation in my investigation to prove everything I had done up to this point was wrong.

We all learned at the same time the recording was provided to TMZ by Riccio. After a few moments of trying to figure out how the recording existed, it became clear there was a hidden recorder in Room 1203 at the Palace Station and Riccio now had the recorder in his possession. My instant thoughts went to my need to get the recording for the case file. It was an important piece of evidence. After a short time, the reality sank in that if the robbery was covertly recorded in the room, then there was probably not enough time to get the recorder out after the robbery and the police arriving. If my assumption was correct, then when the police officers, detectives and crime scene analysts were in the room, they were probably recorded, too.

The Las Vegas Metropolitan Police Department employs some of the most intelligent and dedicated professionals I have ever known and if I ever had a need for their services, I would feel safe and secure in their abilities and professionalism. However, there are times when police officers are removed from the public's watchful eye, they tend to say and do things they would never do outside of being in what they consider a secure environment. There were quite a few law enforcement personnel in Room 1203 during the evening as it was being processed. I had to accept the possibility that individuals from my department were recorded saying some inappropriate things. I knew it was not going to be easy getting those recordings, but there was not a doubt I needed them.

The next morning, Eddie called Riccio in California to ask about the recording. Riccio said he had a recording device in the room from when he checked in until detectives allowed him back in the room after they had processed the room. Riccio also explained he had six other recordings that he covertly made before and after the robbery. Eddie was able to get Riccio to agree to send copies of the audio files to us by mail, which was as good as it was going to get for now. I called Roger to inform him what we had learned. Roger explained that he would need the actual recording device for court. Up until this point in the investigation, I still had my sights aimed at Riccio being a co-conspirator and I wanted to be able to eventually submit an arrest warrant on him for involvement in the armed robbery. Regardless of what I wanted, I understood at this point I would have to trust that Roger knew best how to deal with Riccio because he had something we needed.

Two days later, on Sept. 20, 2007, Eddie received a FedEx package from Riccio. The package was sealed and when Eddie opened the package, it contained a CD with seven audio files. The seven files were labeled 3, 4, 5, 6, 8, 9, and 10. The largest file was file 6, which was the recording of the activities and robbery inside Room 1203. Eddie made a copy of the CD and submitted all seven files to the Robbery/ Homicide Transcription Section to have the audio from the files transcribed. Roger requested that I contact the local FBI to have the CD examined for any editing or tampering. When I called the local FBI office, I spoke with Special Agent Larry Wenko, who explained they could help us, but it would be better to provide them with the original device the recordings were made on. After talking with SA Wenko, who reinforced the need for the original recording device, I was beginning to accept the probability that I would not be able to charge Riccio for his involvement in planning the robbery because the golden egg his goose laid was going to be immunity.

Though we would not know the content of the audio files Riccio sent us for a few days, we did know the part released by TMZ, which Eddie and I transcribed. It took us approximately 40 hours of independently listening to that six-minute section of the audio to record the statements made during the armed robbery:

**Unknown:** Hey, how you doing?

**Fromong:** Let me run, I've got, uh, I'll give you a call back _____.

**Unknown:** What's up, guys?

**Beardsley:** Oh, no.

**Riccio:** Are any of you guys, duh, the law or anything?

**McClinton:** Get off that phone. Get off that fucking phone.

**Simpson:** Don't let nobody out of here.

**Fromong:** Hold on.

**McClinton:**Get off that phone.

**Simpson:**Don't let nobody out of this room.

**McClinton:**I want you to hang up that fucking phone.

**Simpson:**Motherfuckers. Think you can steal my shit and sell it.

**Unknown:**No.

**Simpson:**Don't let nobody out of here.

**Unknown:**Uh...

**Simpson:**You motherfuckers, think you can steal my—

**Unknown:**You ain't talking, mind your own business.

**Simpson:**Look at this shit.

**McClinton:**No, get over there, walk over there.

**Simpson:**Did you think you could sell my shit?

**McClinton:**Get the fuck against the wall.

**Beardsley:**I'm trying to get past you, man.

**McClinton:**Walk your ass over there.

**Simpson:**You think you can steal my shit.

**Beardsley:**Mike took it. Mike took it.

**Simpson:**I know fucking Mike took it.

**Beardsley:**Hey, I'm on, I'm always on your side.

**Unknown, believed to be McClinton:**Search that motherfucker for a gun. Move that chair.

**Simpson:**I always thought you was a straight shooter.

**Beardsley:**I'm cool. I am.

**Stewart:**Stand up.

**Stewart:**Stand your motherfuckin' ass up.

**McClinton:**Stand the fuck up—before it gets ugly in here.

**Simpson:** Don't let nobody out of here. Is it you?

**Riccio:** I, I had nothing to do with it.

**Simpson:** I trusted you, man.

**Riccio:** I, I just, I didn't.

**McClinton:** Bag this shit up. Bag this shit up.

**Beardsley:** O.J., you know where I'm coming from.

**Simpson:** What are you doing with my fuckin' personal shit like this.

**McClinton:** Bag it up.

**Fromong:** I bought it from Mike.

[Inaudible conversation]

**Beardsley:** Mike sold it all, right?

[Inaudible conversation]

Gil–, Gil–, Gilbert, Gil– ... Get it back from Mike.

**McClinton:** Bag it up.

[Inaudible conversation]

**Stewart:** Bag, bag this shit up. Bag it.

**McClinton:** Bag it.

**Stewart:** Bag it.

**Alexander:** What did you bring this shit in, man?

**Riccio:** They said they were friends of yours.

**Alexander:** What did you bring it in?

**Beardsley:** I didn't bring it.

**Unknown, believed to be Simpson:** Bullshit.

**Beardsley:** I didn't bring it.

**McClinton:** I'm gonna ask you one more fuckin' time.

[Inaudible conversation]

**McClinton:** Bag this shit up.

**Riccio:** The bellboy came and got it.

**Beardsley:** Mike. Mike sold this to Bruce, man. He sold it.

[Inaudible conversation]

Hey O.J., Yale knew all about this stuff.

**Simpson:** No, man, Yale didn't know about this shit.

[Inaudible conversation]

He's at the hotel waiting on us right now.

**Beardsley:** No, I'm talking about two years ago. O.J., O.J., I don't have a problem with you, man. Are you mad at me?

**Simpson:** I thought you were a straight shooter, man.

**Beardsley:** I am. I am, man.

**Alexander:** Sitting here with all the shit, he should be mad at you.

**Stewart:** Motherfucker don't even know who we are, do he?

[Inaudible conversation]

He don't even know who the fuck we are.

**Alexander:** What is this right here?

**Fromong:** Well, that's my Joe Montana.

**McClinton:** Hey, hey ... get those balls. Hey, get those fuckin' pillowcases off and put those fuckin' balls in it.

**Beardsley:** Well everything here isn't O.J.'s.

[Inaudible conversation]

**Unknown:** You supposed to be a snitch?

[Inaudible conversation]

**Stewart:** Work with your ass.

**Riccio:** They, they said that they were new to this.

**Stewart:**Is this a motherfuckin'

[Inaudible conversation]

**Simpson:**Bruce I thought I knew.

**McClinton:**Are you fuckin' around? Are you fuckin' around?

**Riccio:**I thought Charlie, I thought Charlie was gonna give you the stuff.

**Beardsley:**O.J., he didn't.

**Riccio:**Charlie told me he was going to give you the stuff.

[Inaudible conversation]

**Fromong:**He called him. He called me.

[Inaudible conversation]

**Simpson:** So where is Mike now? Where does he live?

[Inaudible conversation]

**Fromong:**He lives in Fresno somewhere.

**Simpson:** Where?

**Fromong:**He lives in Fresno.

**McClinton:**Hey …

[Inaudible conversation]

Hey, let's move it.

**Beardsley:**You went on TV.

[Inaudible conversation]

You only met me a couple of times and, you know.

[Inaudible conversation]

**Alexander:**Don't bag it up.

[Inaudible conversation]

**Beardsley:**O.J., I was, you know I was always loyal to

you, you know that, man.

**Stewart:** You all know this shit ain't over with though. It ain't over with.

**Unknown:** Yeah.

**Stewart:** Motherfuckin', fucker.

**McClinton:** You motherfuckers lucky you ain't in LA or your ass would be laying on the floor.

[Inaudible conversation]

Bye, bye.

**Beardsley:** No, Mike is the, Mike is the guy you …

[Inaudible conversation]

**McClinton:** Hey, man, I don't care, I, I wouldn't even be talking to you motherfuckers right now, I'm tellin' ya.

**Unknown:** I'll listen.

[Inaudible conversation]

**Beardsley:** Nobody knows who …

[Inaudible conversation]

**Stewart:** Motherfuckin' jets travel two million miles to get …

[Inaudible conversation]

**Fromong:** If I could …

[Inaudible conversation]

**Unknown:** I hear ya.

[Inaudible conversation]

**Stewart:** This morning a fucking jet.

**Unknown:** I hear ya.

**Stewart:** You know what I mean?

**Riccio:** That's me. That's me, O.J.

**Simpson:**How do I know that you, you motherfucker. You tried to take my fuckin' shirt.

[Inaudible conversation]

**McClinton:**Crack you on the fucking head see how you like that shit, motherfuckers.

**Unknown:**God-damned.

[Inaudible conversation]

**Fromong:**If I could, the Montanas are mine.

**Stewart:**Get that off the covers.

**Unknown:**What this shit?

**Beardsley:**Hey, O.J., are you and I cool or what?

**Simpson:**I thought we were cool, my man.

[Inaudible conversation]

**McClinton:**Hey …

[Inaudible conversation]

shit is over with.

[Inaudible conversation]

**Beardsley:**O.J.? O.J.?

[Inaudible conversation]

O.J., what about that leather jacket?

[Inaudible conversation]

You know?

**Alexander:**Hey, Juice?

[Inaudible conversation]

**Simpson:**You know, you know Mike sold you that fuckin' jacket.

**Beardsley:**I never got it. I thought you still have it. I don't have it. I thought you had it. I tried …

[Inaudible conversation]

**Unknown:**You want, you want them to keep the phones?

**Unknown:**Huh.

**Fromong:**It's just my personal phone.

**Stewart:**Yeah, well, well, you know.

[Inaudible conversation]

**McClinton:**Put your fucking phones on the bed. Put your fuckin' phone on that bed. Put your fuckin' phone in bed. You, too.

**Fromong:**Please don't break it, I just ...

**McClinton:**Hey, man, shut your fucking mouth before you get your ass whooped.

**Unknown:**We'll leave it, we'll leave it at the front desk, OK?

**Fromong:**OK. Thank you very much.

**Stewart:**Leave the phone. Leave the phone. Leave that for the motherfucker's ... This is our job. You're out of it.

[Inaudible conversation]

**Fromong:**O.J., I'll give you Mike's number if you want it.

**Simpson:**Yeah, give me that. Give me that bitch's number. Give me Mike's number. I want Mike's number.

[Inaudible conversation]

**Beardsley:**Hey, O.J., are we, are you and I are cool or what?

**McClinton:**Fuck him.

**Simpson:**I thought we were cool, man.

**Beardsley:**I never got a chance ...

**Simpson:** Hey, here's, here's the motherfucker …

[Inaudible conversation]

**McClinton:** It's time to go.

**Simpson:** Grab that.

**McClinton:** Get that. Let's go. It's time to go.

**Unknown:** What you doing?

**Fromong:** He asked me to get Mike's number.

**Unknown:** Oh, oh.

[Inaudible conversation]

**Unknown:** Write his number down.

**McClinton:** It's time to go. Listen to me. It's time to go. Now! Come on!

**Unknown:** I ain't gonna do …

[Inaudible conversation]

**Fromong:** And if I could—if you could leave the Montana …

[Inaudible conversation]

**Unknown:** Motherfuckers.

**Fromong:** I bought it from Mike, okay? He sold it to me.

[Inaudible conversation]

**Simpson:** What Montana thing of yours they got?

**Fromong:** I'm sorry, what?

**Simpson:** What Montana thing of yours they got?

**Fromong:** They took the box of my Montana lithographs.

[Inaudible conversation]

**Simpson:** Then we'll put them at the front desk.

**Fromong:** That's my baseball bats.

[Inaudible conversation]

Thank you very much.

**Riccio:**He said he was gonna buy it to give to you.

[Inaudible conversation]

**Simpson:**I want these motherfuckers' numbers.

**Riccio:**He said he was gonna buy it to give to you.

**Simpson:**No, grab the numbers. Grab the numbers.

**Fromong:**I'm, that's what I'm doing.

**Alexander:**I'm gonna leave these at the front desk.

**Fromong:**Okay, under …

**Alexander:**What's it under?

**Fromong:**It's under "Gilbert," it's a 559 number.

**Riccio:**They took one of my bags.

The violent nature of what could be heard on the audio recording convinced me that regardless of what spin a defense attorney used to minimize what happened in Room 1203, the bottom line was these men terrorized Bruce Fromong and Alfred Beardsley for six minutes while pointing guns at them and taking their property.

*"One of the stolen signed pictures of O.J. Simpson of his record breaking 1973 season with the Buffalo Bills"*

*"One of the stolen signed pictures of O.J. Simpson and Johnnie Cochran from the day Simpson was acquitted of the murders of Nicole Brown and Ron Goldman"*

*"One of the stolen signed pictures of O.J. Simpson and Al Cowlings when they played together for the San Francisco 49ers"*

*"This is a picture taken of the stolen property when I recovered it on September 17, 2007, during the arrest of Clarence Stewart"*

*"The cart being pulled by the bellmall at the Palace Station is carrying Bruce Fromong's property to room 1203 where it would soon to be stolen by O.J. Simpson and his men during the armed robbery"*

*"Charles Ehrlich and Charles Cashmore are recorded by Palace Station surveillance cameras carrying out stolen property after the armed robbery"*

*"O.J. Simpson and Michael McClinton are recorded by Palace Station surveillance cameras leaving after the armed robbery. Simpson is carrying Alfred Beardlsey's sunlasses and hat which were taken from Beardsley during the armed confrontation."*

*"Clarence Stewart recorded by Palace Station surveillance cameras carrying out stolen property after the armed robbery"*

*"O.J. Simpson and his men meet up with Tom Riccio in the Palace Station lobby before Riccio led them back to room 1203 where the victims were waiting. From left to right – Michale McClinton, O.J. Simpson, Tom Riccio, Clarence Stewart, Walter Alexander."*

*"Alfred Beardsley, Tom Riccio, and Alfred Beardsley walking back to room 1203 where Fromong and Beardsley believed they would be meeting a buyer for Fromong's memorabilia collection."*

*"These are the guns recovered at Michael McClinton's residence during the service of a search warrant."*

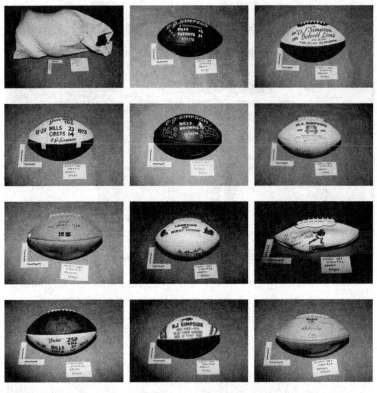

*"These footballs were recovered when I arrested
Clarence Stewart on September 17, 2007."*

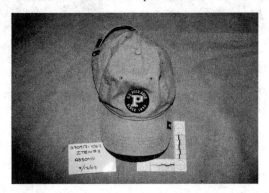

*"Alfred Beardsley's hat recovered when I arrested Clarence
Stewart. This is the hat O.J. Simpson is seen carrying
out of the Palace Station after the armed robbery."*

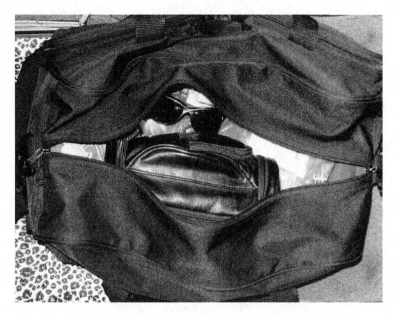

*"Alfred Beardsley's sunglasses recovered pursuant to search warrant being served on Walter Alexander's luggage when Eddie and I arrested Walter Alexander on September 15, 2007. These are the sunglasses O.J. Simpson is seen carrying out of the Palace Station after the armed robbery."*

*"Joe Montana lithographs recovered when Eddie and I arrested Charles Cashmore on September 19, 2007."*

# OFFICE OF THE DISTRICT ATTORNEY

**DAVID ROGER**
*District Attorney*

**CHRISTOPHER J. LALLI**
*Assistant District Attorney*

**TERESA M. LOWRY**
*Assistant District Attorney*

**MARY-ANNE MILLER**
*County Counsel*

October 21, 2008

Sheriff Gillespie
400 Stewart Ave.
Las Vegas, NV 89101

RE:    State of Nevada v. Orenthal James Simpson

Dear Sheriff Gillespie:

I am writing to commend Detective Andy Caldwell for his work on the above referenced case.

On September 17, 2007, Detective Caldwell was assigned to investigate a robbery which took place at the Palace Station Hotel and Casino. Detective Caldwell conducted a thorough investigation which resulted in the arrest and conviction of OJ Simpson and five (5) other individuals.

Detective Caldwell spent hundreds of hours listening to and analyzing audio and video recordings of the crime. According to the jury, the audio tapes were the most important evidence in the case.

Additionally, Detective Caldwell allocated much of his own time preparing for his testimony. At trial, Detective Caldwell provided truthful and thoughtful testimony and impressed the jury with his professionalism. Due to his diligence and commitment in investigating the matter, the defendants were convicted of all counts.

In sum, Detective Andy Caldwell is a model investigator who is a credit to the Las Vegas Metropolitan Police Department. I was grateful for his assistance and look forward to working with him on future matters.

Very truly yours,

*KanyeRoser*

DAVID ROGER
District Attorney

DR/kjk
cc: Det. Andy Caldwell

*"After O.J. Simpson was convicted, District Attorney David Roger sent this commendation for me to Sheriff Doug Gillespie who was the Sheriff of the Las Vegas Metropolitan Police Department during this time."*

# CHAPTER 11
## MORE ARRESTS

The next morning after hearing the recordings on TMZ was Tuesday, Sept. 18. It was my last scheduled day off for the week and Rod had offered us to take the day off, but Eddie and I agreed we needed to come in. I did not want to slow the momentum we had built up.

I got into the office at about 9 a.m., and about 45 minutes later, I received a call from Fromong's wife, Lynette. Fromong had suffered a heart attack and was in critical condition at Cedars Sinai Hospital in Los Angeles. Lynette said he was under a tremendous amount of stress after the armed robbery and all the media attention and collapsed. Lynette was upset as she was telling me what happened. I was at a loss for words. I hurt for her. I asked her to keep me posted and to let Bruce know he was in my prayers.

Within moments, I received another call from Howes, the Florida attorney. He wanted to make arrangements for his client, Charles Ehrlich, to turn himself in. Howes could not have called at a worse time. I had just heard the audio recording of how the suspects in this armed robbery terrorized Fromong and Beardsley and gotten off the phone with a wife whose world had been turned upside down as a result of what Howes' client was involved in. It was not a good time to talk with an attorney. I asked Howes if I could call him back in a few minutes and he agreed. I took a few minutes to gather my thoughts and then gave him a call.

Howes wanted to know if I would allow Ehrlich to make a statement before I decided what charges to arrest him for. There was a frustrating aspect of the various suspects turning themselves in through their attorneys; they almost look like they are doing the right thing. Between the pressure of search warrants being served, suspects being arrested, media attention and now the armed confrontation being played for the world to hear, they are not doing the right thing. They're simply trying to avoid being arrested at a place and time that they believe is inconvenient. There is nothing voluntary about these suspects turning themselves in. Just like their actions throughout their crime, they are thinking about how to best serve themselves. I understand Howes was trying to do the best he could for his client, but I needed to do what was right for the case and for the victims. I explained to Howes that I would be more than happy to meet with his client and take a statement from him, but he would be booked on the same charges that his co-defendants were booked for. Howes was not happy with my response, so I told him I did not care if his client turned himself in or not, but if he didn't, I would blow up a picture of his client and put out a media release for all to see. Howes abruptly ended our conversation.

The robbery section was still receiving various tips about the identity of the remaining suspects who had not been arrested. Most of the tips appeared to be without merit, but they still needed to be investigated in order to be fully ruled out. Some of the tips could be ruled out with some simple records checks and others required a few phone calls.

As I was working through the tips, I received a call from attorney Bill Terry, a well-respected defense attorney in Las Vegas, who told me he was representing McClinton. Terry asked if I had time to take his client into custody at 3 that afternoon, which worked well for me, so I agreed. At this point, completing the arrest paperwork was just a matter of copying and pasting the facts and circumstances from the last person arrested and adding the details of the next arrest. I was still advising Roger when I made an arrest, but there really was nothing new to brief him about with McClinton's arrest. I decided it would be better to have an arrest warrant for McClinton just in case he did not show up at the 3 p.m. appointment. I applied for the arrest warrant, which was granted. Eddie and I arrived at Terry's office at about 3:20

p.m. His office was also located in an older residential part of downtown that had been converted into a business area. As we walked in, a receptionist greeted us and took us directly back to Terry's office. His office was older than Lucherini's, but it was still nice. There was definitely a contrast between the two attorneys' offices. Lucherini's seemed pretentious, like he was trying to impress people, while Terry's seemed confidently pragmatic. Terry met us halfway between his door and desk with a handshake. McClinton was quietly sitting in front of Terry's desk. Terry introduced us to McClinton. I asked if he was going to be giving a statement and Terry said McClinton would not at that time. There was not much more in the way of conversation. I placed McClinton in handcuffs and had him follow me out to my vehicle.

McClinton was placed in the front passenger seat and Eddie sat behind him. It was a short distance between Terry's office and the Clark County Detention Center, less than a mile. I intentionally didn't ask McClinton any questions while we were in the car to create an even more uncomfortable situation for him than already existed under the circumstances of his arrest. I think McClinton tried to break his perceived uncomfortable silence by telling me he was a good person and talking about O.J., saying Simpson "caused all this." I did not inquire beyond his statements because he was in custody and represented by an attorney.

On the day after I arrested McClinton, Roger told me Terry had a recording McClinton made that I needed to pick up. I'm not sure why Terry did not mention the recording when I arrested McClinton, but my guess was that he tried to use it as leverage to work out a plea deal with Roger. I drove over to Terry's office with Eddie and Terry gave me a microcassette tape. I broke out the two plastic tabs on the cassette to prevent the recording from being recorded over and then Eddie placed the cassette into a player. The recording was too scratchy to make anything out clearly. I submitted the recording to our transcriptionists, who did not have better luck with being able to make out what was on the tape.

After this tape was enhanced by the FBI, it would prove to be a valuable piece of evidence.

On the morning of Sept. 19 at about 9:45 a.m., Lt. Paul Page called me, saying he'd heard from a friend and private investigator, Robert Lawson, regarding another Palace Station suspect who wanted to turn himself in. Lawson told me he worked for attorney Robert Miley, whose client, Charles Cashmore, was involved in the robbery with Simpson and wanted to turn himself in to me at Miley's office. I grabbed two pictures from the surveillance video at the Palace Station of the two unidentified suspects. I was not sure which one of the two outstanding suspects from the picture this was going to be. I talked a big game to the attorney who called from Florida, but the reality was I did not have a positive identification on either of the two remaining suspects. Eddie and I jumped in my car and drove down to Miley's office. Like Lucherini's and Terry's offices, Miley's law firm is in the nice older residential neighborhood where homes had been converted into small businesses. Miley's office was nicer than the other buildings in the area; it had been had been completely remodeled and looked like a modern office building. His office stood out; it looked more professional than the other buildings and gave me the impression he was more successful than the other attorneys in the area.

Of the two males seen the surveillance video, one was a little heavier than the other. When I walked into Miley's office, I could clearly see Cashmore was the heavier of the two. Miley did not want Cashmore to offer a statement at this time, but he did want to turn in stolen property. Cashmore had the autographed Joe Montana lithographs as well as Fromong's cell phone. A crime scene analyst recovered the property and Cashmore was transported to the Clark County Detention Center, where he was booked accordingly.

It was easy to gather from various comments made by

Alexander and Simpson that one of the suspects was not as well known by the rest of the suspects. It was clear Cashmore was the one who was the outsider.

It was not until Oct. 1, 2007, that Cashmore would offer a statement in exchange for a plea bargain detailing his involvement in the armed robbery. If there was one suspect who was in over his head, it was Cashmore.

Cashmore explained that he was an out-of-work member of the culinary union who had known Stewart from a previous job. Stewart had reached out to Cashmore about getting a job at a Louisiana nightclub. Stewart told Cashmore to meet him at the Rio Hotel and Casino to talk about the job and meet a couple other guys involved in the nightclub. During the day, before the armed robbery, Cashmore interviewed with the two men and then called Stewart, who was supposed to be at the interview. Stewart told Cashmore he was running late to the meeting and told Cashmore to go across the street to the Palms, where he could meet O.J. Simpson. Cashmore did not want to pass up an opportunity to meet O.J. Simpson, so he went over to wait for Stewart. Cashmore went out to the Palms pool area, walked up to Simpson and introduced himself, mentioning he was there to meet up with Stewart. Simpson offered Cashmore a drink and let Cashmore take some pictures with him.

Stewart was almost at the Palms, so Cashmore walked out to the valet area with Simpson and another man who Cashmore only knew as "Charlie" to wait for Stewart. Cashmore was hoping to get some work by bartending at the wedding Simpson was in Las Vegas for. He claims he did not know anything about Simpson going to get property back, that he was just there hoping for work and enjoying an opportunity to hang out with O.J. Simpson. When Stewart pulled up, some people got out of the vehicle. Simpson and Charlie got into the vehicle, so Cashmore followed. It was not until they were driving off that Simpson and Stewart started talking about going to go pick up some memorabilia.

They asked Cashmore if he would help carry stuff. Cashmore felt like he was just helping out and the thought of something illegal going on had not even entered into his mind.

Stewart dropped off Cashmore and Charlie at the main entrance of the Palace Station while Stewart and Simpson went to go park the vehicle. They were going to meet up at the hotel front desk. When Cashmore and Charlie met back up with Simpson and Stewart, there were two guys there in suits who Cashmore did not know. Cashmore said there was discussion about Charlie going to a room to verify the property in the room. He claimed he started to feel like something was not right when Riccio arrived.

After talking for a few moments, they all started walking toward the hotel area. I asked Cashmore what he was thinking and he said, "Be honest with you, I don't know what the fuck I was thinking. I mean it's like what the hell is all this for if he's going to get his own stuff, why, why is there, you know it went from four of us to carry to stuff, which I could understand, to two guys with suits that just pop out of nowhere. I mean I'm common sense smart enough to know maybe that's not the right, something's not right."

Cashmore was caught up in the moment and he described everything happening fast. When they arrived at Room 1203, Riccio opened the door and walked in, followed by Cashmore and Charlie, when they were pushed out of the way by the other suspect. Cashmore described the chaos as he remembered it: "I see O.J., you know, in, in, in Beardsley's face, you know, MF-ing him, in his face yelling at him, blah, blah, blah, blah, blah. Um, at that point in time, I mean it was just got crazy. Then I, then you know he's cussing mad about being a friend, you know da-da-da. I don't know the conversation until I heard the tape, be honest with you. It was so much going on. Um, I hear, you know at that point in time McClinton has his gun out at that point."

He described Stewart "friskin' " Fromong and throwing him against the wall while the guys in the suits were yelling.

"You know telling everybody, up against the wall. You know, 'If this was L.A., everybody be dead,' you know, or, 'You'd be laying where you lie,' and shit like that. And at this point in time, that's when I'm pretty much scared shitless, you know, and I, I mean the whole event was so quick. From here they're talking and then I remember him saying frisk everybody, take cell phones ... the conversation got really bad. The guys with the gun, you know, everybody's hollering at one time, scream, blah, blah, blah, blah, blah. Then he orders ... these ... he orders the victims, purple suit orders victims to box it up how you brought it. Repeats it three or four different times. You know, 'Motherfuckers,' you know, 'Box that shit up. Box that shit up.' Then I step up, I don't want anybody to get hurt, Charlie and I, he turns around to us, says, 'Box that shit up. Get that shit boxed up.'"

Cashmore explained he was scared and did not want anyone to get hurt, so he started packing up the property in pillowcases and carrying it out of the room. He did not know about Beardsley's sunglasses or hat being stolen, but said one of the other suspects gave him the cell phone and he (Cashmore) was supposed to drop off the phone at the front desk, which he neglected to do. They took all the property out to Stewart's Navigator and loaded it. As they drove back to the Palms, he described Simpson telling people on the phone there were no guns. Cashmore remembered Simpson telling people there were no guns multiple times, saying it in a way that Cashmore thought he was trying to get everyone to agree and get their story straight so everyone would say the same thing if they got questioned by the police.

When they arrived at the Palms, Simpson looked at the property and said he did not want anything that was not his. Cashmore took the Joe Montana lithographs and the cell phone, which he was going to take back to the Palace Station front desk, but never actually did. He did work as a bartender at the wedding the next day. The other suspects were also at the wedding, where he had the opportunity to talk with

Stewart.

Stewart, who was mad at Simpson, implied he intended to keep the memorabilia to sell it and split the money. Stewart told Cashmore to keep what he had as payment for bartending because he probably would not get any other pay. Cashmore held onto the property until he turned himself in to his attorney.

I'm not one who is often sympathetic to criminals, but as I sat across the table from Cashmore, I did feel sorry for him. He deserved whatever punishment the courts gave him, but he truly was sucked into a bad situation because he was infatuated by a fallen superstar. Cashmore was the unfortunate product of a society that idolizes people like O.J. Simpson, Woody Allen and Michael Jackson—of a society willing to overlook major character flaws in charismatic individuals because of a talent to perform in front of others. As my investigation progressed, I came to accept the reality of some people having a twisted infatuation on O.J. Simpson. I think it is normal for most people to have a moment of being star-struck. However, I believe for most people it is not rooted in infatuation, but rather in a cultural curiosity to see a person from TV in real life. And that moment of being star-struck often passes with recognizing celebrities are just like anyone else.

After we had arrested Cashmore, we all went back to the robbery office. An unidentified person called the robbery office and claimed to have information about a suspect we were looking for named Charles who lived in Florida. The call was forwarded to Linda. The person on the phone insisted on remaining anonymous, but wanted to provide information about someone named Charles who was believed to have been involved in the robbery with O.J. Simpson. The caller did not have Charles's last name, but did provide a phone number and some criminal history that was verified. Linda remembered a man named Charles having checked into the Palms with the wedding party. Linda called the Palms and was able to get the last name of Ehrlich for a man named Charles who checked in with O.J. Simpson.

I had not put much effort into getting a positive identification of the last subject because everything was happening so fast. Even though I had an attorney from Florida calling about a subject turning himself in, I did not know exactly who the attorney was calling about. With the hotel registration, Linda was able to get Charles's date of birth and Social Security number. Linda contacted the Miami-Dade Police Department to obtain a photo of Ehrlich, which was a match for my last outstanding suspect.

Now knowing who Ehrlich was, I called the phone number given by the anonymous caller. A male answered the phone, identifying himself as "Charlie." I told him who I was and that I was calling about his involvement with the armed robbery at the Palace Station with O.J. Simpson. I told him I had spoken with Howes, who claimed to be his attorney and had told me Charles wanted to turn himself in. Charles did not say much, so I continued on by telling him if he wanted to turn himself in, he had better do it fast because I have him identified and I would be submitting for an arrest warrant in the next couple of days. If he did not turn himself in, I would have him extradited back to Nevada. Ehrlich responded well to my warning by saying he had been in contact with John Moran, an attorney in Las Vegas, and was working out a time to turn himself in on the 20th or 21st. I called Moran's office and asked what his plan was with Ehrlich. Moran explained that Ehrlich would be turning himself in at Las Vegas Justice Court 9 at 7:25 a.m. on Sept. 21.

I decided to obtain an arrest warrant anyway, just in case Ehrlich changed his mind.

While I was in the process of arresting the remaining suspects, O.J. Simpson was still being held in jail without bail. On Sept. 19, 2007, O.J. Simpson had his first court appearance in Las Vegas for a bail hearing. I knew from talking with some of my friends at the Clark County

Detention Center that Simpson caused unusual difficulties at the jail. His fame resulted in other inmates wanting to see him and talk to him; a simple of move of Simpson down a hall would cause other inmates to gawk and holler at him. There was little doubt in my mind that he was going to get a bail set so he would be able to get out of custody to await his trial. At the bail hearing, Judge Tony Bonaventure agreed to the terms negotiated between Roger and Simpson's attorney, Yale Galanter. Simpson was released on a $125,000 bail. He had to surrender his passport; have no personal contact with the victims, witnesses, or co-defendants in the case; and agree not to travel outside of the country. Simpson posted his bail amount that day and was released from jail.

On Sept. 21, Eddie and I were waiting at Justice Court 9. Ehrlich's name was on the court calendar without having been arrested or charged, which told me Ehrlich's attorney was trying to get him in the court system for his involvement, but at the same time, get a bail hearing so he would not have to go to jail. I had never seen or even heard of someone trying to do that. I informed the prosecutor in the court that I had an arrest warrant for Ehrlich, who was not in the courtroom yet. Ehrlich walked in with his attorney and I instantly recognized him from the surveillance video at the Palace Station. The judge called Ehrlich's name and ordered him to be arrested for his warrant.

The criminal courts in Las Vegas are located in the Regional Justice Center, which is just east of the Clark County Detention Center, with a tunnel connecting them. The tunnel goes under the street that divides the two buildings. This is how inmates are taken to and from their court appearances. After arresting Ehrlich in Justice Court 9, Eddie and I took him through the underground walkway to be booked for his arrest warrant. Ehrlich did not say much, but while we were riding the elevator from the floor the court was on to the basement, Ehrlich looked up at me and said, "I knew I shouldn't have come to the wedding."

Like Cashmore, both McClinton and Ehrlich eventually gave statements to work out plea deals with the DA's Office in which they detailed their involvement in the armed robbery with O.J. Simpson. McClinton worked out a deal and gave his statement on Oct. 10, 2007, before the Nov. 8 preliminary hearing. Ehrlich held out longer and did not work out his deal until after the preliminary hearing. Ehrlich gave his statement on July 30, 2008, just before the trial was set to start. The statements given by Alexander, Cashmore, McClinton and Ehrlich were generally consistent in their various accounts of what happened the day of the robbery at the Palace Station.

Alexander, Cashmore, McClinton and Ehrlich entered into agreements with the prosecution and pleaded guilty for their involvement. The agreements required honestly testifying at all criminal proceedings involving the co-defendants. Their guilty pleas were entered into prior to the start of the jury trial, but their sentencings did not happen until after the trial was over—to ensure they did, in fact, testify honestly.

Without question, the best deal was arranged for Alexander, who admitted to having a gun during the robbery. His deal was the best because he was the first to cooperate. Alexander pleaded guilty to conspiracy to commit robbery, a B felony, which had a potential sentence of one to seven years in prison, but the prosecution was going to request probation. Part of the plea agreement spelled out that even though Alexander and the prosecution agreed to these terms, the actual sentencing was entirely up to the sentencing judge. If the judge did not sentence Alexander to probation, Alexander had the right to withdraw his plea and ask for a jury trial.

Cashmore, whose involvement was partially a result of being a celebrity sycophant and partially being in the wrong place at the wrong time, received the second-best deal. Though he pleaded to a lesser crime than Alexander, Cashmore did not have a gun. Cashmore pleaded guilty to accessory to robbery, a C felony with a potential of probation or one to five years in prison. The agreement between Cashmore and the prosecution was that the prosecution would not ask for prison, leaving Cashmore's sentence entirely up to the sentencing judge with no option, as Alexander had to withdraw his plea if he did get sentenced to prison.

McClinton agreed to plead guilty to conspiracy to commit robbery and robbery, both B felonies. The conspiracy charge had a potential sentence of one to six years in prison and the robbery charge had a potential sentence of two to 15 years in prison. McClinton also agreed to forfeit his firearms. The prosecution agreed not to ask for a prison sentence, but if the sentencing judge did sentence him to prison, the prosecution agreed to recommend that the sentences run concurrently. Basically, if the sentencing judge sentenced him to two years in prison for the conspiracy and two years in prison for the robbery, then the prosecution would request both two-year sentences be served at the same time, with McClinton serving two years total. Without the request for the sentence to be served concurrently, the sentence could be served consecutively (back to back), which would result in being in prison for four years (in this example).

Ehrlich, who was the last to enter into a plea agreement, did not accept accountability for his actions until after the preliminary hearing. As a result, his deal appears to be the worst of the four, and rightfully so. One of the most frustrating aspects of police work is how suspects try to find loopholes to avoid being held responsible for their actions. Even though Ehrlich was not armed and was not specifically accused of any violence, he agreed to plead guilty to two felonies. Ehrlich pleaded guilty to attempt accessory to robbery, a D felony, and attempt burglary, a C felony. The attempt accessory to robbery had a potential sentence of one to four years in prison and the attempt burglary had a potential sentence of one to five years in prison. As with

McClinton, the prosecution agreed not to ask for a prison sentence, but if the sentencing judge did sentence him to prison, the prosecution agreed to recommend that the sentences run concurrently.

After I finished the paperwork to book Ehrlich into jail, I received a call from Lynette Fromong, who said Bruce's condition was improving and that he was out of the critical care unit. The next call I got was from Roger, who said his office had made arrangements with Riccio to turn over the original recording device. Roger needed Eddie and me to head to Los Angeles as soon as possible to get the device from Riccio at his home.

# CHAPTER 12
## RICCIO RECORDINGS

Roger had already contacted my chain of command and explained to them the importance of recovering Riccio's recording device as quickly as possible. By the time Roger called me, he already had our out-of-state travel approved. Eddie and I had booked Ehrlich at jail and I needed to go back to the office first to put Ehrlich's paperwork in the case file. With traffic, I knew it was going to be at least a five-hour drive down and probably four-and-a-half to five hours back, so I wanted to get going. After putting the paperwork in the file, Eddie and I loaded into my unmarked Nissan Maxima for a day trip to Los Angeles and back.

It was still early in the morning on the 21st, only eight days after the armed robbery at the Palace Station. As I pulled onto Interstate 15, I turned on a sports radio station and they were talking about O.J. Simpson. I think I would have probably listened to the same program even if I weren't involved in investigating the case, but there is no doubt I found it more interesting because I was involved in the case. My interest was not based in hoping to learn new facts or information, it was in how successful Simpson's defense was at getting out this nonsensical narrative about Simpson only taking his own property back. It was a mix of callers who hated Simpson and wanted him to go to jail for anything and other callers expressing their thoughts of how stupid it was that people were making such a big deal about him just taking back what was rightfully his.

I knew from people in my personal life that this little twist of the truth that Simpson told the world through the Associated Press about some of the property belonging to him and that there were no guns used had some traction. I found myself answering questions from friends who didn't understand why he was arrested for robbery if he was getting his own property back. I also found that when I had a chance to explain what the facts I had learned during the investigation, every person I spoke with who had questions changed their opinions and agreed that he should have been arrested.

I knew neither one of us were going to want to listen to talk radio and hear the news entertain the stories about O.J. taking his own property back. So after a few minutes, I switched the radio over to a Christian radio station and Eddie just laughed at me and told me, "No way are we listening to this all the way to L.A." I didn't think it was going to fly, but I figured I might as well try. There might be some police officers who eat, drink and sleep everything police, but neither Eddie nor I are that way. Even though we were on the clock working, we were on a road trip and if we didn't have to talk about police stuff, we weren't going to. We both have daughters who are close in age and have similar interests and we often went ATV riding together. We always had things to talk about.

As we dropped down into Rancho Cucamonga, I mentioned to Eddie that it was all city the rest of the way in. I was born and raised in Fraizer Park, a small mountain town north of Los Angeles, so I was familiar with the L.A. area. Eddie was from back east and had never been to Los Angeles, so I don't think he was expecting city that far away from L.A. We were fairly fortunate because we were headed into L.A. in the early afternoon, so traffic flowed pretty fast. We got off the freeway at about 2:30 pm.

I was relying on my GPS to get me to Riccio's house. As we wound up a few residential streets, I made my final turn onto Riccio's street. The only people who knew Eddie and I were on our way were Roger, his staff and Riccio. Yet somehow, the entire network and cable press machine knew we were coming. His residential street was packed with massive news trucks with their satellites and cameras already set up. There was not enough parking on his street, so I had to drive past the media vans. I am sure they saw my Nevada license plates and knew we were there to talk with Riccio. By the time I parked, a few of the reporters had got out of their trucks and started walking toward Riccio's driveway. Eddie and I walked directly to his driveway and past the reporters. They were asking us questions, but there was nothing to say. The reporters stayed off Riccio's property, but they stayed outside even after Eddie and I went in. Riccio and another man came to the door and Riccio invited us in. Eddie instantly asked Riccio, "Why did you tell the news we were coming?" Riccio said he didn't tell anyone we were coming, which was complete baloney, but it wasn't worth the argument. We went into Riccio's living room, where there were two other men—his attorneys—waiting. Because of the visible tension between Riccio and me, Eddie did most of the talking.

Riccio gave us the Olympus digital recording device, as well as an old cassette tape labeled "O.J. Mess #2," a personal check he had written to Beardsley dated September 2004, and a business contract between Riccio and Beardsley dated October 2004. It was during this meeting that Riccio explained how he commonly records people when he makes deals with them involving memorabilia. He wanted to give us the cassette tape, check and contract to show that he had done business with Beardsley in the past without any problems. While we were at his home, he also showed us other tapes he had where he recorded conversations to document verbal agreements between him and other parties.

This was when I learned about a deal Riccio had made with Simpson, which he claimed was the reason for the recordings. The different stories about this detail can get a little convoluted and while it is important to have the truth, I don't believe I was able to ever get the complete truth on what Riccio was about to explain. Riccio claimed he was contacted by Beardsley, who was looking to sell high-end O.J. Simpson memorabilia that used to belong to Simpson.

Riccio knew O.J. Simpson had lost the rights to his book "If I Did It" and that it was still going to be published by the Goldmans, which meant Simpson was not going to get money from the book. Riccio figured he could make a substantial amount of money from selling copies of the book published by the Goldmans in the memorabilia world if Simpson would agree to exclusively sign copies for Riccio.

Riccio reached out to Simpson and offered to tell Simpson about Beardsley trying to sell O.J. Simpson memorabilia, which Riccio felt Simpson would want to get back. In exchange for connecting Simpson with his lost memorabilia, Riccio asked Simpson to exclusively sign 200 books, which Riccio claimed that Simpson agreed to do. The wedding of Simpson's friend in Las Vegas was already set for the second week in September, so that was the date Simpson wanted to set up the meeting. Though Riccio did admit to setting up the meeting, he consistently denied knowing they were going to have guns and take property by force.

Remember that Fromong claimed Beardsley contacted him and Beardsley claimed Riccio contacted him. Riccio's recordings showed there is some truth in Riccio's explanation that he was contacted by Beardsley and without Beardsley, there would have never been a reason for Riccio to contact Simpson. Riccio arrived in Las Vegas and went to the Palms to meet with Simpson. The first of the seven recordings Riccio's recorder had stored on it was marked as File 3, which contained a recording of Riccio meeting with Simpson in a public place at the Palms with other people around. In that recording, there are a number of statements that gives Riccio's story some credibility. As Riccio talks about the meeting to take place later that evening, Simpson talks about how a man by the name of Mike Gilbert had helped Simpson move some valuable property after he lost the civil lawsuit and was ordered to pay over $30 million to the families of Ron Goldman and Nicole Brown.

During the process of moving the property, it is alleged

that Gilbert took a large amount of property that Simpson claimed to be his. At some point, Gilbert was required to complete paperwork for the California courts about allegations of him possessing any property of value belonging to Simpson that should be turned over toward the payment of the settlement against him. In the following conversation, he makes clear his understanding of Gilbert claiming to the courts that he does not have any of Simpson's memorabilia:

**Simpson:** So, so he got, like, four thousand pictures of [inaudible].

**(Unknown):** So pictures and stuff.

**Simpson:** So, he called me and said, "Now, I don't feel right about your personal stuff." Right. So he's pretending he's buying it, you know, this is Charlie. Charlie gonna be there as a buyer cause the guy has …

[Inaudible conversation]

The guy has had two turn over orders from the state of California saying he had none of my stuff. I kept saying he stole my stuff. So he quietly tried to get him to sell it quietly, you know, for a guy that don't want, don't want the Goldmans involved. So they gonna meet tonight. I'm gonna show up with a bunch of the boys and take the shit back. They can't do nothing about it.

[Inaudible conversation]

Can't tell the police … [inaudible]

**(Unknown):** [Inaudible] doesn't exist.

**(Unknown):** You already told them it didn't exist.

**(Unknown):** All right.

**Riccio:** He don't want to show it to anyone in California, either.

**(Unknown):** Yeah.

**(Unknown):** But then ... [inaudible]

**Simpson:** [Inaudible] ... turn over order [inaudible] turn over order [inaudible] anything you had of O.J.'s.

**Riccio:** [Inaudible] wants to know where you want to do it here. You wanna do it in the Horseshoe (Binion's Horseshoe) where they're still at?

**(Unknown):** How can they bring it?

**(Unknown):** Where do they have it?

**Riccio:** They have it. They have it. It's all in one van; everything fits in one van.

**(Unknown):** So are they gonna pull it out of the van?

**Riccio:** What else they gonna do, show it all over the room?

The conversation went on to talk about Gilbert being there and Simpson confronting him about taking his property.

The next exchange takes place on the digital recording file marked File 4 in Simpson's suite. This conversation took place after Riccio met with Simpson in the public place on File 3 and before the armed robbery. Here it becomes clearer that Riccio is recording Simpson to get him to say he will exclusively sign the books for Riccio.

**Riccio:** He went, he went and looked on the internet. Uh. And I called the ... your house. They were gonna give it to me 47 percent off the cover price of the book. If I bought a hundred 'em, 40 percent, 7 percent cover book. All $13 somethin' like that. And, uh, but they're sayin', the warehouse is sayin' they don't even have 'em yet. So I'm thinkin' they're thinkin' it's gonna be another week or two before it comes out.

[Inaudible conversation]

So I mean, I [inaudible].

[Inaudible conversation]

He, he sells [inaudible].

**Simpson:** They had a big pre-order on Barnes & Noble [inaudible].

**(Unknown):** Yeah.

**Simpson:** Everybody's predictin' even Oprah that they would get endorse it.

**Riccio:** I, I, I might do a sale through my auction.

**Simpson:** [Inaudible] we all felt that the first week it would sell. And then it would fall off. Cause it got people [inaudible] just [inaudible] crazy wanna know [Inaudible].

**Riccio:** Well, we, we...

... We might do a Dutch auction through our auction and advertising through our auction. And that's in the beginning of November for the [inaudible]. As long as we know that you ain't do nothin' with nobody else.

**Simpson:** I ain't doin' nothin'. You ain't got to worry [inaudible].

**Riccio:** So O.J. gave us his word. He ain't doing nothin'. He's only gonna do it with me. And nothin' like a week or two weeks. But you're definitely gonna do it with me.

**Simpson:** Now, I mean you gonna reach a day where ... there ... some many of my fans will buy the book.

**Riccio:** But like you just said, you hit you hit the needle in the head.

**Simpson:** [Inaudible] in order for me to sign it [inaudible].

**Riccio:** You can't wait. You can't wait a long, long time [inaudible].

**Simpson:** [Inaudible] You can wait enough because it's like it makes it like [inaudible]. I mean, the public thinks

I'm not signin' the book. It makes the cost of me signing. And you say I got a hundred books signed or he's gonna sign a hundred of 'em for me ...

**Riccio:** All right.

**Simpson:** ... it's gonna make the price go up.

**Riccio:** So we gotta [inaudible] O.J. ... It's gonna be, it's gonna be two

[Inaudible conversation]

**Simpson:** [Inaudible] nobody else.

**Riccio:** Ya ain't doin' it for nobody else. It's gonna definitely do it [inaudible].

[Conversation overlaps]

I, I, and he's gonna do it for [inaudible] this what I want.

I want this book cause I know I have people already askin' me. And I told 'em I can get it done. So, so I, I think maybe [inaudible]. I think maybe a limited edition 200 at first. We'll see how it goes and maybe we'll do more later.

After listening to this recording, Riccio's involvement became a little more understandable; he simply saw an opportunity to make money. A little later in the same conversation, we heard that Riccio did not want a violent confrontation.

**Simpson:** [Inaudible] once we get the shit, we, you and I'll sit down [inaudible].

**Riccio:** All right.

**Simpson:** We're gonna get it away from there and put it in my man's truck, he's gonna take it and, uh [inaudible]. First of all these guys gotta be stupid if they don't just back off.

[Inaudible conversation]

**Riccio:** I'm thinkin' probably like I said, 75 percent chance that they're just gonna back off.

**Simpson:** Yeah.

**Riccio:** I don't know … I don't know what else could happen after that.

**Unknown:** I mean you think, I mean I don't think, how's the guy gonna argue with him directly. Ya know what I mean.

**Simpson:** [Inaudible] he's got my stuff [inaudible].

**Unknown:** Yeah.

**Simpson:** [Inaudible] Beardsley knows that Mike stole it from me. Beardsley knows that.

**Unknown:** And he knows [inaudible].

**Riccio:** Yeah. They're sayin' that you owed 'em money.

**Simpson:** [Inaudible] shit.

**Unknown:** I know.

**Unknown:** Yeah. Yeah. I think it'll go all right.

**Simpson:** [Inaudible] every gig I ever did for Mike, Mike got paid. Mike paid me.

[Inaudible conversation]

[Laughter]

**Simpson:** So how do … I don't fuck him outta money.

The context of the full audio paints a clear picture of Simpson believing Gilbert was going to be in the room and a conviction that the items he believed was going to be in the room belonged to him. In the context of the conversation, he also indirectly acknowledges there is a substantial amount of valuable property being hidden from being turned over to pay toward his legal obligation. As I listened to these audio files, it became apparent that in his greed and desire to avoid accepting the court's decision of his liability in the deaths of Ron Goldman and Nicole Brown, Simpson engaged in deceitful behavior with slimy people who figured out there was nothing Simpson could do if they started selling off his old memorabilia.

In the digital audio recording File 5, Riccio meets up with Beardsley at the Palace Station before the robbery. In the conversation, you can tell Riccio believed Gilbert was coming and would be the one with the property. It sounds like this is the first time Riccio had heard the name of Bruce Fromong and it is when Riccio learns Beardsley misled him. Up to this point, I believe Riccio thought the property being brought to the room was more personal in nature not just sports memorabilia. Beardsley initially talks about the property being brought to the Palace Station that night as items that were at one point in Simpson's personal trophy room, but then Beardsley slowly introduces to Riccio the reality of the property being brought by Fromong as being impersonal memorabilia like autographed photos.

**Beardsley:** This is, uh, between you and I, this is, uh, stuff O.J. personally loves. And it was in his, uh, in his trophy room in his house. But the fucking try to pay his goddamn bills.

**Riccio:** Let me ask you this. If I can get a hold of O.J., would you be interested in, in buying this later on for him?

**Beardsley:** He has no money.

**Riccio:** He has no money.

**Beardsley:** No money. And he doesn't pay anybody. That's why he's in this situation. I was supposed to bring this stuff down to Florida to him a few years ago and Mike Gilbert said, "Come over to my fucking house and it'll be out on the front lawn."

**Riccio:** This guy knows Mike Gilbert.

**Beardsley:** He knows him?

**Riccio:** Ah, he heard of him or something. I mentioned his name …

**Beardsley:** I know he was the manager for years.

**Riccio:** He said, he …

**Beardsley:** And Mike says, "It'll be in my fucking, it'll be on the fucking front lawn come and get it." So… I's gonna go up there with some guys. Mike wanted to fight with me cause, uh, I was talking to O.J. and he, Mike and, uh …

**Riccio:** Well, wha-, what kind, what kind of like, you're gonna, you're gonna give him a receipt with this. You wanna not give him a receipt.

**Beardsley:** [Inaudible] give him a receipt.

**Riccio:** Right. What, is this coming from Mike Gilbert?

**Beardsley:** Well, here's the deal. This is Mike Gilbert's best friend, uh, the guy that's got it.

**Riccio:** [Inaudible] another one, you know what.

**Beardsley:** Well he's got a lot, he's a wealthy, prominent guy. He helped start Mounted Memories and [inaudible].

**Riccio:** I know Mounted Memories.

**Beardsley:** He does a lot of signing. Very [inaudible].

**Riccio:** What's his name?

**Beardsley:** Bruce Fromong.

**Riccio:** Bruce Fromong?

**Beardsley:** And, uh, and told Bruce today I said, "Well,

after today I know, I know probably you guys are going to be dealing with each other on other stuff. Cause he's always doing signing with, with big guys, you know. He does, ah, Super Bowl parties.

**Riccio:** I mean, I do more with people that are, like, like, you know what I do? When I, when I ...

[Talking over each other]

**Beardsley:** [Inaudible] high-end shit, man.

**Riccio:** Know we're experts in? Know what we're experts in? Like celebrity, a lot of them are deceased. Contacts, checks, documents.

**Beardsley:** We got the contracts, but Mike, see Mike always had money problems. He never could hold on to a buck and, uh, Bruce, you know, Bruce is a pretty prominent guy and they're best friends. And they've, and, uh, Mike just kept borrowing money from Bruce, and Bruce wound up with everything. So, uh ...

**Riccio:** Is Mike going to be here today?

**Beardsley:** No, no, Mike's out of the picture, period. He's got a regular job now.

**Riccio:** So this guy Mike isn't going to come to us now and say it's his?

**Beardsley:** Mike's out. Mike's out of the business, he's working. He's got, I guess he's back on his feet. He wants nothing to do with O.J., doesn't even want to hear his name. Uh, O.J., Mike turned down a million dollars to write a book, you know, cause he's loyal to O.J. and O.J. fucked him. Left him over 20 grand. Mike was getting evicted from his house. He called up O.J. and saying how he needed 25 hundred bucks, they're gonna evict me and family. And O.J. said, "Hey, man, you're on your own, can't help you." That's what started it all. O.J. wouldn't, uh, O.J. got weird, man.

**Riccio:** Didn't they, didn't they do like millions of dollars in business together?

**Beardsley:** Yeah, Mike did [inaudible].

**Riccio:** Now they're all, now they're all broke.

**Beardsley:** Uh ...

**Riccio:** After making millions. I mean, I went through a few hundred thousand, uh ...

**Beardsley:** Like there will be these books that he's bringing. They've never been released. Never put out on the market. They're leather bound, uh, copies of the book you sold the guy. [Inaudible]

**Riccio:** I had, I had cases of those books I bought from ... you wouldn't want to hear what I paid for them.

**Beardsley:** No leather bound.

**Riccio:** With a certificate from, from the [inaudible] and everything?

**Beardsley:** Yeah and these, these were signed in jailed, um ...

**Riccio:** I mean, I'll take more but it, it ...

**Beardsley:** They were, they were all sealed.

**Riccio:** It would have to be, unless I can maybe sell him something. We'll sell him retail. But for me, I'll take 'em all, but it'd have to be cheap. I buy anything, dude. I have a warehouse full of crap. As long as the price is right. I'll buy. I'll buy.

**Beardsley:** [Inaudible] he told me it was gonna be over for 50 bucks apiece [Inaudible]

**Riccio:** I'll buy [pause] I'll buy piece.

**Beardsley:** [Inaudible] he can't even get Pete Rose to sign, uh.

**Riccio:** No, no. I, no I won't pay 50 bucks a baseball

unless he writes, what'd I tell you he wants writing.

**Beardsley:** What, I'm sorry, I bet on baseball.

**Riccio:** He does it. He writes that on it.

**Beardsley:** And he charges extra for that. I know. I got a bat signed like that.

**Riccio:** You get.

**Beardsley:** I had five. I bought five of 'em.

**Riccio:** I'll do several thousand dollars worth of business on that alone. Oh, you got him to get I'm sorry, I bet on baseball.

**Beardsley:** [Inaudible] but, but these are laser …

**Riccio:** 'Cause he will. Dude, I know he will.

**Beardsley:** These are laser, laser inscribed and signed.

**Riccio:** Oh, no, they gotta be signed by him. Sorry, I bet on baseball and I have a market for those. I've sold 'em through my auctions.

**Beardsley:** He's selling them on his own website. He's got his own website [Inaudible].

**Riccio:** I could sell more than what he can sell them for. But I may, I'll buy, I'll buy quantities of 'em from him. I'll buy dozens of 'em. He's gotta write ...

[Talking over each other]

**Riccio:** Only way for me to make money on Pete Rose and I can make money, is it's got to be, "Sorry I bet on baseball before."

**Beardsley:** You gotta to talk to Bruce on that man. He'll hook you up with him.

**Riccio:** He's coming here today, too?

**Beardsley:** He's coming at six. He's bringing the stuff.

**Riccio:** So how did he get a hold of all the stuff …

Mounted Memories from Mike?

**Beardsley:** Well, he used to, uh, he used to be one of O.J.'s managers, too, in the past and he used to, uh, when O.J. was having trouble during [inaudible] he would cash checks for him [inaudible].

**Riccio:** So, so what do we here? We got, we got plaques, we got suits.

**Beardsley:** Uh, the suit (the suit O.J. Simpson wore the day he was acquitted of the murders of Nicole Brown and Ron Goldman), he's not bringing the suit. He's gonna, that's not to be brought out at a different time since it's in storage somewhere.

**Riccio:** Yeah, he told the client [inaudible].

**Beardsley:** It's 400 bucks to get out here.

**Riccio:** Why?

**Beardsley:** It's in a fucking vault. [Laughs]

**Riccio:** Why does it cost, cost, didn't me, didn't cost me four—

**Beardsley:** It's in hiding. It's in hiding.

**Riccio:** —hundred dollars to get out here. It's gonna cost the suit 400 dollars to get out.

**Beardsley:** Well he'll explain. You know, the, the suit is, uh, that would have been something for your auction house to handle, but I don't think O.J. would have liked you doin' it.

**Riccio:** Uh, plus, plus.

**Beardsley:** [Inaudible] have a relationship with him now, right?

**Riccio:** Well, I, I, I've done a deal with him. I don't really have a relationship, relationship. I've, you know, I've done a deal with him. I did a signing with him a couple years ago. I mean he's not like, we chat on the phone every day or anything like that. But I could probably ...

**Beardsley:**He never want, see he, he's pissed that he's not getting any money out (of) that suit and he claims that Mike ripped him off on the suit, which Mike didn't do. O.J. gave it to Mike the day he got out of jail. And he, he didn't know what he was doing. He just gave it to Mike. Mike stored it and, um, knew one day it was going to be worth money. We've been going back and forth on that suit for years, you know, to decide when it was going to be sold.

**Riccio:**So what do we got here today? What's coming at six?

**Beardsley:**All the presentation balls, the plaques, awards, uh, court-worn ties, uh, all kinds of signed photos. I just told him to bring the signed photos just in case the guy wants 'em. With O.J. and his Heisman and shit. Court-signed stuff.

**Riccio:**Court-signed stuff. What's that mean?

**Beardsley:**Photographs from court.

**Riccio:**Oh.


Though the recordings do seem to corroborate Riccio's explanation of why he was covertly recording the meetings surrounding the armed conflict at the Palace Station, they also establish that the plans as he knew them were unraveling and he did nothing to stop the meeting that led to the robbery. The recordings also reveal that though Riccio did not make the initial contact that started the ball rolling on the meeting at the Palace Station, he did start to push the ball faster and manipulate its path for personal gain. The importance of all Riccio's recordings cannot be overstated. Even a cursory listening of the recordings provides remarkable insight into how some people are still in awe over O.J. Simpson, how at times Simpson can have a jovial and charismatic personality, and how Simpson can shift from seemingly normal to a greed-based, anger-driven rage without notice.

While the truth is important here, it is not necessarily relevant to the actual crime. I know this might sound strange, but as far as my investigation was concerned, it did not matter if Riccio contacted Beardsley or if Beardsley contacted Riccio. It did matter that neither Riccio nor Beardsley planned for anyone to come into Room 1203 with guns and take personal property from another person using force or the fear of force.

Because of Simpson's notoriety and past public lifestyle, it is interesting to know about property that might be connected to him. It is interesting to know if Gilbert and Fromong were involved in various schemes to hide property for Simpson to avoid being held accountable for what a court assigned him legally responsibility for. It is interesting to know who was backstabbing who and what they thought they would gain from it. But for as interesting as these details might be, they do not change anything about what happened in Room 1203 on Sept. 13, 2007. This knowledge simply helps provide insight to the character of the people involved. It helps to understand why this was done at night in a small hotel room. The bottom line is, if Simpson and his crew of armed strongmen went into Room 1203 and only took Fromong's cell phone and left all the other property, the resulting arrest and charges would have been identical. If a robber goes into a bank where he has an account with his money and with a gun, demands all the money from his account and only takes $1 from the cashier, he still has committed armed robbery.

The danger for me as the investigator in this situation was to avoid getting caught up in the schemes of the people involved. Simpson and his men used guns to steal West Point memorabilia, Joe Montana memorabilia, Pete Rose memorabilia, Fromong's cell phone and Beardsley's hat and sunglasses, along with hundreds of signed O.J. Simpson photographs that Fromong could prove he owned. The couple of footballs and plaques involved in this hide-and-seek game was not a relevant factor in this criminal act.

The digital recording marked File 6 was the longest of the files. Riccio had turned it on and placed it on top of the large clothes cabinet in Room 1203 before he brought Beardsley and Fromong into the room. The cabinet was over six feet tall and had a decorative top, which allowed for Riccio to place the recorder in a place no one—not even the police—would look for a recording device under these circumstances. I don't believe Riccio planned to leave the recorder in the room, risking it being found by police, but he never had a chance to recover the recorder once the police arrived without an officer or detective seeing him grab it. If we had located the recorder, we would have seized it as evidence and Riccio would have lost out on selling it to TMZ. It was this file that contained the audio of the actual robbery and hours of law enforcement personnel working in the room. Some of the comments made by law enforcement personnel would be brought up at trial, but the totality of the comments recorded all pointed to the reality of the robbery.

File 8 was a recorded phone conversation between Simpson and Riccio the day after the robbery while Riccio was home in California. Riccio can be heard trying to be friendly to Simpson, but still telling him that he was not going to lie about there not being guns involved. After having some experience with Riccio, it is my opinion that Riccio was still concerned with getting Simpson to sign the books for him, so he did not want to upset him, but he had to tell Simpson he would not lie about the guns.

**Riccio:** Listen, I gotta tell ya something, man.

**Simpson:** Okay, go ahead.

**Riccio:** I gotta tell ya something. Listen to me.

**Simpson:** Yeah, yeah.

**Riccio:** The thing they're coming down on a lot is there's a guy there, I don't know whether you saw it. I'm thinking maybe you didn't see it. Probably didn't see it. But there was a guy there with a gun.

[Talking over each other]

**Simpson:** I [inaudible] with a gun.

**Riccio:** I know. I know you didn't see it. I know you didn't see it.

**Simpson:** I didn't see it.

**Riccio:** But, I mean I, I, I, I, you know. They, you know, they were saying that they saw it and I saw it, too. And I couldn't, and I'm not going to lie about that. You know, they, they, they'll you know what I mean. I can't lie about anything. But, but …

**Simpson:** Absolutely didn't see [inaudible]

[Talking over each other]

**Riccio:** But, I know, I know, I know, I can tell from talking to you, you didn't see nothin'. But, I'm telling you.

**Simpson:** These guys walked out the door. I didn't see it.

**Riccio:** That's the whole, I mean, it, it, it, it …

**Simpson:** Hold on, hold on, hold on. How much, OK. All right. I didn't see … [Inaudible]

**Riccio:** I, I know, I know, I know you didn't.

**Simpson:** The guy walked in before me.

**Riccio:** I know, I, know, I know you I know you didn't see it.

**Simpson:** I told everybody to back off. I said, "Back off, man." And then I talked to the guys.

**Riccio:**Right.

File 9 was another phone call between Simpson and Riccio after the robbery. Again, in this recording, Riccio seems to try and keep on Simpson's good side with a focus on a future business relationship.

**Simpson:**[Inaudible] Tommy, I'm just sick but let me say give me ...

**Riccio:**No, they're digging shit up and they're ruining my business right now.

**Simpson:**... just give me 40 seconds. When you, call me and what you said to me is, you didn't try to make money this. You said whatever they're saying that you just tell the truth. And you tell the truth and that's no problem, I'd tell everybody. You became, you went up in my eyes. I don't know what business you'll do. But I will for free sign anything to you from this point on. Because you could have made money with these fucking assholes. And you didn't ... and, and ...

**Riccio:**Well, let me tell you ...

[Inaudible conversation]

Maybe I'm gonna happen, maybe I'm gonna hope that you became a hero again like you were when I was a kid. And, and, and I can, uh, work for you, because I don't know if I have a job anymore.

**Simpson:**Yeah, I know the day when things started to change. [Inaudible] Oh, no, this stuff, was abs— absolutely [inaudible] stole from O.J., and that the point people gotta realize is that you di—, you weren't there tryin' to make money ...

**Riccio:**No, but let me tell, can I tell [inaudible] happened.

File 10 was the last of the recordings from Riccio. It contained another phone conversation between Riccio and Simpson in which Simpson tries to convince Riccio that he did not see a gun in the room. Riccio gives Simpson some wiggle room by consistently saying how he understands how Simpson could have not seen a gun, but that Riccio did, in fact, see at least one gun.

Once I had the recorder back in Las Vegas, I again contacted Special Agent Wenko about having the recordings enhanced and evaluated to see if they were edited. I took the device to SA Wenko, who took custody of the recorder. He also advised me of a potential six-month turnaround time. I called Roger back and informed him of how long it would take and he asked me if I could also find a private company to also enhance the audio files. After doing a substantial amount of research, I located a company named Professional Audio Labs, owned by Paul Ginsberg, who had done work on many high-profile cases and had been previously contracted by various federal, state and local law enforcement agencies. Ginsberg appeared to be the best in the business. I contacted Ginsberg by phone and he was willing to work on the recording I had from Riccio. He also promised a two-week turnaround. I sent him copies I made from the CD Riccio had mailed to us prior to driving out to Los Angeles to pick up the recorder.

The audio files recorded by Riccio were instrumental in my investigation. The recording of the violent six-minute confrontation was shocking enough to keep my focus on the crime that occurred inside Room 1203. That focus helped me to not get too caught up in the dishonest narratives created by defense attorneys and the media to try and persuade the public into thinking this was a business transaction in which property was returned to its rightful owner. No matter what angle a person views the facts of this case from, the end result is seeing an armed robbery. Some might suggest that Simpson going to prison for this robbery is like Al Capone going to prison for tax evasion, but just as Capone did, in fact, not pay his taxes, Simpson did, in fact, commit an armed robbery.

# CHAPTER 13
# PRELIMINARY HEARING

I knew I would not have too much time to get as much work done on the case as possible because there would be a preliminary hearing within a few weeks. When I made the initial arrests, Roger wanted me to provide each person arrested with a notice of intent to seek an indictment, which gave the prosecution the option of taking the case quietly to a grand jury. Within a week, I knew this case would not be heard by a grand jury and it would be proceeding through the more common process of a preliminary hearing. The nervous part of me wanted this case to go to a grand jury because those proceedings are done in private without cameras.

A preliminary hearing is like a mini-trial in front of a judge without a jury. The goal at the preliminary hearing is simply to establish there are sufficient facts to proceed to a jury court trial. Preliminary hearings are public and I knew the moment the DA's office made the decision to have a preliminary hearing that this case was going to bring with it intense media scrutiny. I knew the case was solid, but I also knew if the case drifted away from the facts of what happened in Room 1203, then it became confusing and difficult to see it for what it was.

I knew from experience that the defense team would do everything it could to point away from the actual robbery, to highlight the oddities of the victims and witnesses and point to the odd circumstances that led all the parties to meet in Room 1203 that evening. My nerves were shot when I heard about the preliminary hearing. I had a case on Court TV in 2005, I had been around the filming of "COPS" and I had a case on "America's Most Wanted." I knew that they would all pale in comparison to the attention of this preliminary hearing.

Knowing the preliminary hearing would be just around the corner, I buckled down on tying up loose ends. There were small twists and turns in this case just like any other. However, in this case, small twists oftentimes made their way into the news. I was contacted by Special Agent Dave Neider from the Los Angeles Field Office of the FBI who had information about Riccio. On Aug. 21, 2007, Riccio reported to SA Neider that he was contacted by O.J. Simpson about Simpson wanting to set up a "sting" to get back some of his memorabilia that had been stolen from Simpson years ago. Riccio did not have details about where or how Simpson was going to do the sting; he just wanted to make sure he told someone. SA Neider did contact the Los Angeles police department to see if anyone had any information about stolen O.J. Simpson memorabilia, but there was nothing further that could be done with the information Riccio provided. The fact that Riccio did not have any further details about what Simpson's plans were was evident in the conversations Riccio recorded between himself and Simpson on the day of the robbery, before it actually happened. SA Neider emailed me his investigative report, which detailed the contact he had with Riccio. It was good information for me to know, but based on the information Riccio provided, there was no way SA Neider could have known where it was going to happen, when it was going to happen, or that it was going to be a violent armed confrontation. Riccio did not follow up with SA Neider to inform him it was going to happen on Sept. 13, 2007, nor did he mention it was going to happen in Vegas. The investigative report SA Neider provided to me would later be discovered by the media and made into national headlines that implied the robbery in Las Vegas was preventable.

In tying up loose ends, there was also some maintenance that I needed to do—the same maintenance I tried to do in all my cases. I called Fromong multiple times to check on his medical condition, which was steadily improving. Once he returned to Las Vegas, Eddie and I met him at his house to learn more about how his business worked. I also recovered his cell phone from the evidence vault, where it had been impounded since Cashmore was arrested, and returned the stolen cell phone to him. Fromong showed us other O.J. Simpson memorabilia and more of the same signed pictures that had been stolen during the robbery. He explained that Simpson gave some of the memorabilia and other property was given to Gilbert. That property was then stored in a storage locker and later given to Fromong. This was true only for fewer than 20 of the hundreds of items stolen from Fromong in Room 1203. The rest of the Simpson memorabilia was items he designed or had printed and paid Simpson to sign. The West Point, Pete Rose and Joe Montana memorabilia had nothing to do with Simpson. While we were there, Fromong played a voicemail Simpson had left for him on Sept. 15, 2007, at 10:12 a.m.:

"Ah, hey, Bruce. [Inaudible] Uh, some of [inaudible] your things are mixed up in my stuff [inaudible] get it back to ya. So how do I get it back to ya? So, uh, let me know where to, uh [inaudible] gonna meet up, uh, to get it. This, uh, ya know, I don't want none of your stuff. Only my stuff. In any [inaudible] uh, you can call me at 305-XXX-XXXX, 305-XXX-XXXX. Hey, look [inaudible] the police are handling what's goin' on with that. But, uh, don't give my number to anybody. I'm not gonna give your number to anybody. [Inaudible] Uh. [Inaudible] asked me to get [inaudible] stuff that you had mixed up in my stuff [inaudible]. 'K? All right, buddy. I ain't stealin' nobody stuff. [Inaudible] I'm just a little upset that you guys stole my stuff. [Laughs] All right."

The date of the call was troubling to me: two days after the robbery and the implication of what Simpson said was he knew they had Fromong's property. He also appears to be making this the victim's fault: "stuff that *you had* mixed up in *my stuff*" (italics added for emphasis). After blaming the victim, Simpson ended the call by making sure the victim, from whom he violently took property at gunpoint, knew he was still mad at the victims: "*I'm* just a little *upset* that *you guys stole my stuff*" (italics added for emphasis). In my experience, these kinds of statements are part of the gaslighting method commonly used by abusive and controlling individuals. "I was mad because she did not clean my house." "She took my car." "I told her she could leave, but she could not take my stuff." Abusive individuals try to make their victims assume some responsibility for why the abuser had to hurt them.

It was during the preparation for the preliminary hearing that I met Chief Deputy District Attorney Chris Owens, who was going to be prosecuting the case with Roger and would become my primary contact while working through the rest of the investigation. Owens was the team chief over the district attorneys who handled murders and the more high-profile cases. He was a very soft-spoken man, but also very quick-witted, which sometimes would catch me off guard because he was one of the oldest prosecutors I had ever worked with. Owens was the go-to guy in the office for advice. Eddie and I could be in his office working on the case and not more than 15 minutes would pass between prosecutors on his team coming in the office to ask his opinion about a case or to update him on the status of a case. I learned a great deal from watching him interact with others; his calm and positive demeanor was infectious and encouraging. Owens did not get worked up about too much and he was good about staying focused on what mattered in a case. He also had a pleasant way of insisting that I continually work on the audio from this case, transcribing it and correcting it as my ear became more and more in-tune with the contents. He was the driving force behind Eddie and me spending day after day working on the audio we had in preparation for the preliminary hearing, which was scheduled for Nov. 8, 2007.

Weeks after I had received the information about Riccio contacting the FBI in Los Angeles from SA Neider, it became an issue the media was interested in. On Nov. 2, 2007, I was sitting down for dinner at home when my department-issued cell phone rang. It was Ken Ritter from the Las Vegas Associated Press office. I thought it was strange that he had my phone number, but then he explained he had called Lt. Clint Nichols (who was my lieutenant at the time) to ask if it was true that the FBI was contacted by Riccio to report Simpson setting something up to get his memorabilia back.

I initially told him I could not comment about an ongoing investigation. Ritter started reading off to me what sounded like SA Neider's report and told me he just wanted to confirm I had received it. Under normal circumstances, I would not talk with a reporter, but he told me Lt. Nichols gave him my cell phone number and told him to call me. One of my biggest regrets was telling Ritter I had received the report. He asked if the FBI had passed on what they learned before the robbery or after. I responded by explaining they contacted me after the robbery and gave me their reports. There was no way they could have known to contact the Las Vegas Metropolitan Police Department before it happened because there was no way to know when, where or if the crime was going to take place.

On Nov. 3, 2007, the front page headline of every major newspaper in America read, "FBI knew about Simpson's plan." As I was headed into work that morning, I saw a copy of the *Las Vegas Review Journal* with that headline, so I picked up the top paper and started to read the article. The headline was so incredibly misleading, but it definitely made me want to read the paper. I combed through the article to see if I was quoted because if I was and with that misleading of a headline, I knew I would hear about it from our department staff. There were three sentences that referenced me and when I read them, I wanted to pull my hair out. The journalist half-quoted me and changed the context of our conversation.

*Las Vegas Police Det. Andy Caldwell, the investigator handling the case, said Friday the FBI did not alert his department before the confrontation between Simpson and collectors Alfred Beardsley and Bruce Fromong in a room at a Las Vegas casino hotel. "They contacted us afterward and provided us with the documentation," Caldwell told the AP. He said he had no information about any FBI investigation into the incident and said he has no idea about the nature of the contact between federal agents and Riccio or why they were talking with him.*

Ritter did not finish what I said about how there was no way they could have known to contact my department, instead he ran with, *"They contacted us afterward and provided us with the documentation,"* and ended the quote with a comma. The half-quote made his headline sound so much better, though. And while I did say I didn't know about the nature of the contact between Riccio and the FBI, the context was that I wasn't there and therefore, it was not my place to say anything. I did get a phone call that day from my department's Public Information Office to tell me I should refer all future media questions to their office. It was a hard lesson learned and it made me gun shy about discussing this case with anyone even after it was over.

Part of my problem with Ritter's article seemed to be symptomatic of the investigation; no one wanted this to be the simple armed robbery that it was. Most people wanted there to be this amazingly dramatic back story that either made his actions more egregious or more innocent.

The only other curveball that was thrown before the preliminary hearing came from O.J. Simpson's friend, Tom Scotto. Scotto was the man who got married in Las Vegas on Sept. 14, 2007, and his wedding party was the primary reason

O.J. Simpson was in Vegas that weekend. On Oct. 9, 2007, Scotto called the LVMPD Robbery Section to report that he was contacted by Alexander, who was asking for help. Of course, he had a voicemail recording. I had never experienced investigating a crime where most of the suspects, victims and witnesses knew each other at some level and called each other leaving voicemails. It created an unusual paradox; it was helpful in that I had more evidence to work with, but it was also detrimental because I understood the reality of the opportunistic nature of the people who were involved in this case. There is little doubt in my mind Scotto had more contact with the other suspects and witnesses than this voicemail from Alexander, and the only time I was going to be told about these encounters is when it benefitted Scotto's agenda. It was clear Scotto felt this voicemail benefitted his agenda:

Wednesday, Oct. 3rd at 9:33 a.m.
Hey, Tom, this is, uh, this is the Golden One, partner. Um, you told me to call you if I need some help. I need some help, man. You know, and if I can get some help. I don't have to hit no bills or nobody. I haven't as of yet, so I mean, um, if I can have some help to fight, then I won't have no problems wondering if they had, that my friend, you know, but, uh you know I, I was angry and this shit just came down. But now, uh, if I got some help then, uh, I'll do whatever I can. And I think I can do quite a bit. So, uh, give me a call when you get the kids.

When Scotto played this message for me, I had the opportunity to also interview him over the phone. I asked Scotto what type of help he felt Alexander was looking for and he told me he believed Alexander needed money.

Scotto's opportunistic nature came shining through in my interview. It is important to note Alexander had accepted a deal to testify about what really happened during the robbery and Stewart was not accepting a deal and was not testifying about what really happened in the room. I asked Scotto if Alexander was the only other suspect involved in the case who had contacted him. His response raised a red flag in my mind: "So far, yes."

It's not just the words people say that matter, it's also how they say those words. When I asked if he had been contacted by any of the other suspects, I knew I was asking a broad question and I was going to analyze every aspect of how he answered. If there was no unusual pause and a simple "yes" response then I probably would have just moved on, but he paused for a moment and he qualified his answer with "so far." He was lying and I knew all I would have to do was probe a little deeper and I would get more information out of him. I had already learned he and Simpson were friends, so I started there. I asked, "Okay. Has Mr. Simpson contacted you at all?" Scotto admitted that Simpson had also been in contact with him since the robbery. After a minute or so, I asked, "Okay. Um, so he's the only defendant that's actually contacted you that you're aware of?" After further probing, Scotto then explained Stewart had also contacted him asking for money. I was able to discern from my interview how Scotto felt it was not necessary to report Stewart asking for money because, as Scotto put it, Stewart was a "good guy."

It was easy to read between the lines of what Scotto was saying: Alexander was honest and accepted responsibility so he was *not* a "good guy," while Stewart was dishonest by omission and was trying to avoid accepting responsibility for his actions so he *was* a "good guy." As a police officer, that kind of backwards reasoning made my skin crawl. It gets exhausting dealing with the scum of our society who have convinced themselves that dishonesty should be celebrated and honesty should be labeled as snitching and it should be avoided at all costs.

The irony of Scotto's attempt to "snitch" on Alexander because he was not a "good guy," displayed Scotto's fundamental misunderstanding of what mattered in my investigation. Nothing he told me changed what happened in Room 1203 when Simpson and his friends violently robbed Fromong and Beardsley at gunpoint. At this point in the investigation, there was not much that anyone could say to change what I had learned happened in that room at the Palace Station. Simpson's involvement in this crime had turned a simple investigation into an overcomplicated gathering of windbags.

Transcribing the audio recordings was a tedious task and for the week or two before the preliminary hearing, my primary function was that of transcribing. The audio was often poor quality and conversations were held while other conversations were happening in the background. Some of the more complex moments on the audio recordings could take a couple of hours to identify the voices and conversations in just one minute's worth of recording. Eddie and I sat in a room at two different computer terminals. The computers had a set of foot pedals that controlled play, pause, fast-forward and reverse. Eddie and I would work on different audio recordings then would switch to double-check each other's work. The more I listened, the more I was able to pick up on in the recordings. The transcriptions added remarkable value to the recordings; if you played the audio without reading the transcript, the recordings were at best difficult to understand and mostly impossible to understand.

In the couple of days leading up to the preliminary hearing, I was working with Owens on reviewing the investigation. Testifying in court was not something I was comfortable with and, for the most part, my being uncomfortable was rooted in my unfamiliarity. At that time in Clark County, our system of criminal justice was very fast paced; the vast majority of suspects arrested pleaded guilty based on an agreement between the prosecutor and defense prior to a preliminary hearing, which results in officers or detectives not needing to testify.

Testifying in court is not something officers or detectives receive much training on and though it might seem simple to just sit there and answer questions, there is so much nuance to being questioned. Many defense attorneys are able to solicit half-truths in order to manipulate answers to benefit their clients. An example is errors in paperwork. A defense attorney might go on and on about how well-trained and experienced a detective is, how the detective normally does amazing work, then the attorney will find an error in a report such as the wrong date or a transposed name and now the detective was sloppy and maybe intentionally sloppy. When the defense is questioning a detective, the attorney may deny the opportunity for an explanation, when the explanation clears up the muddy water the defense is so desperately trying to create.

Owens explained his goal of just having me testify for the investigation during the preliminary hearing. It was better for him to have the fewest investigators testify to avoid giving the defense the opportunity to make something out of nothing because I might say we went to California on Wednesday and Eddie might say we went on Tuesday. Though it would be a simple mistake made by one of us, it creates a need for clarification where it did not need to exist. Eddie was with us as we went through the investigation and as Owens discussed what were the relevant facts for the preliminary hearing. Owens was annoyingly confident in my knowledge of the case and when I asked him what direction he thought the defense would go, he would consistently say, "You know the case and you'll do fine." Make no mistake, his kind words only provided brief moments of comfort. I knew I was going to be the one testifying on national television. I wanted to be prepared as best as I could be and Owens was not helping me.

Eddie was no help with my nerves, either, with his repetitive "better you than me." Normally, in a robbery case, the victims and witnesses bear the bulk of the responsibility in establishing what happened when it comes to testifying in court. Most of the time, detectives help to clarify details and provide how the suspects were identified. I knew between the victims and the suspects who had worked out deals with the DA's office that what happened in the room would be covered in detail before I took the stand. While I wanted to be familiar with the entire case, my primary focus was on the recordings and being able to explain their content. I had read the victims' statements, witnesses' statements and suspects' statements. I had reviewed the audio, looked over the evidence and was as prepared as I could be.

By Thursday, Nov. 8, 2007, only six weeks had passed since the armed robbery. Rod, Eddie and I were all under subpoena to testify in the preliminary hearing. At about 8:30 a.m., Eddie and I drove down to the court. The traffic from our office to the court was not bad until we got about two blocks away from the courthouse. As we got closer, we found streets closed off by barricades and traffic officers from our department. The normal parking lot where I parked for court was completely filled by media vans and trailers. The sidewalks around the courthouse were full of people walking around. There were people holding "FREE O.J." picket signs, a person walking around in a full yellow chicken outfit with a sign that read the same and a woman wearing roller skates dressed in a rabbit costume with a sign that read "Stop police brutality." The most interesting person walking around was a guy in a wooden barrel with the same "FREE O.J." sign.

We had to park in a parking garage one block away. Eddie and I were both wearing suits, which was a little more formal than either of us was used to. As we walked around to the entrance for law enforcement and court officers, actual media booths were set up. Power cords ran in all different directions and the buzz of generators powering up all the media equipment could be heard all around. I was doing pretty well with the media trucks filling up our normal parking lot and the crazies holding the "FREE O.J." signs gave me a moment of levity, but when I saw the media booths, I started to get nervous. Luckily, I had a good friend for a partner and as we walked through the area in front of the media, he chuckled and said, "You better not mess this up."

Eddie and I walked through the security checkpoint and into the main atrium of the courthouse. We walked directly to the courtroom, which was on the first floor, and met with Roger and Owens just outside the court for a moment. They were busy and there was not much for us to talk about. We could have sat in the courtroom for the initial part of the hearing, but I knew the defense would invoke an exclusionary rule and Eddie and I would have to get up and leave anyway, so we didn't even look in the courtroom.

The atrium area was fuller than normal. Judge Bonaventure was using a courtroom on the first floor to facilitate the large crowds that were anticipated; he also provided an overflow courtroom in the next courtroom over from his for additional interested parties to watch on a live feed monitor. Eddie and I walked away from all the commotion and sat to watch from a distance. Within a short time, Rod joined us.

There was this moronic notion that I heard being kicked about in the media that revolved around the premise of the prosecutors trying to correct a miscarriage of justice with O.J. Simpson. The absurdity of that line of thinking toward the prosecution at a preliminary hearing has secondary implications of believing Simpson should never be accountable for any crime he commits ever again; if that notion for the purpose of this prosecution were true, then we might as well give Simpson some form of diplomatic immunity and let him commit crime at will. Now if someone wanted to argue that point about the punishment, then they might have a little more support. But the claim of correcting a miscarriage of justice falls short with sentencing, too, because Simpson's defense team refused serious discussions of plea bargains. There was no conspiracy here. It was an armed robbery.

Some would also suggest that Simpson's culpability should be mitigated due to the victims and witnesses having questionable backgrounds and a belief of the co-defendants being dishonest to receive reduced sentencing. There are two simple thoughts that need to be explored in these attacks on the investigation. First, Simpson is the one who chose to associate with the individuals involved in this investigation; Simpson had some form of relationship with everyone involved except Cashmore. Second, the co-defendants all had consistent explanations that were consistent with what the victims and witness reported; each one who accepted responsibility for his actions also confessed to many felonies. And, of course, the co-defendants worked with the investigation in an attempt to get a reduced punishment that is a fundamental facet of investigating crime; citizen cooperation is verified before it is used and to suggest otherwise is a foolish endeavor.

This case was solid and simple: if it did not involve O.J. Simpson, this preliminary hearing would have only lasted a couple hours. Instead, it dragged on for two days.

At one point during the hearing while Eddie, Rod and I were out in the atrium, I noticed a commotion by the courtroom doors. Two bailiffs were escorting a female out of the courtroom, but we were too far away to hear the conversation. There was an area where Simpson's friends were sitting out in the atrium and when this commotion kicked up, Scotto was already sitting on a bench in that area. The female who was escorted out of the courtroom was a younger brunette dressed in a tight mini-skirt and high heels. As she walked away from the bailiffs, she walked over to Scotto and sat on his lap. I assumed this was the woman Scotto married in Las Vegas the day after the robbery. Eddie and I walked over to the bailiffs and asked what was going on. They explained that the woman was making comments to the witnesses as they walked by her in the courtroom.

As we were talking to the bailiffs, Mrs. Scotto turned to straddle Scotto on the bench and started kissing him in a sexually provocative way. The bailiffs hurried over to break up their very provocative and public displays of affection. When the bailiffs reached the Scottos, they again had words with her; she got off him and walked away. As Mrs. Scotto walked away, Scotto walked over to where Rod, Eddie and I were standing and introduced himself to us. None of us had much to say to each other, so after a moment of uncomfortable silence, he walked back toward the courtroom.

I did not testify until the second day. The media presence was the same as the first day at the courthouse, but there was a noticeable decrease in O.J. supporters inside and out. I believe there was a reduced interest once the basics of the case were learned from the first day. It was still an unnerving environment for me because I did feel pressure to not mess up, to not embarrass my department and to not make a fool of myself.

When it was time for me to testify, one of the bailiffs came out into the hallway and called me in. As I walked into the courtroom, my attention was instantly drawn to the floor, where there were cables running from side to side and front to back. As the bailiff walked me to the witness stand, my mind drifted to the importance of not tripping on the wires. The sounds of cameras clicking could be heard from both sides of the courtroom. As I walked onto the stand, the bailiff asked me to remain standing and the court clerk swore me in by asking me if my testimony was true. This couple of moments gave me time to slow my breathing and to try and calm my nerves.

As I sat down, the court clerk asked me to state my name and spell my last name for the record. This process took one to two minutes, but I was still nervous. Owens questioned me, asking about my training, experience and where I worked. He then gave me the opportunity to explain my response to a reported robbery at the Palace Station Hotel and Casino on

Sept. 13, 2007. Every few moments, he would ask a follow-up question, clarifying details about my initial investigation. I walked through my initial response, contacting the victims and witnesses, discovering evidence, identifying suspects, the arrests and the recordings. The defense attorneys did not have many questions for me, which is not unusual for a preliminary hearing. The defense seemed to focus on the recordings and how I knew who was talking during the robbery. This seemed like a pointless direction for them to be pursuing; nothing they asked changed what was heard on the recording of the robbery. After being on the stand for an hour or so, I began to get a little more comfortable and before I knew it, there were no more questions from the prosecution or the defense. There was little doubt in my mind the judge was going to conclude there was sufficient evidence to move to a jury trial, which is what Judge Bonaventure found.

For as quick as my testimony was over in this hearing, I knew this would not be the case at the jury trial. The trial was initially set for April, which meant I had five months to wrap up the investigation. This would be no problem if O.J. Simpson were not involved, but his involvement overly complicated things. For the purpose of my continuing investigation, I saw a huge win coming out of the preliminary hearing; the windbags who were putting so much effort into blowing the sails of trying to make this armed robbery look more complex than it was lost much of their steam.

# CHAPTER 14

# BUILDING UP TO TRIAL

Having a trial date in April was a little quicker than I would have liked. Though the nuts and bolts of my investigation were mostly put together, I knew the trial was going to be completely different from the preliminary hearing. I knew I needed to tighten up every aspect of the investigation. This meant Eddie and I needed to go over everything with a fine-tooth comb to find any problems. One of the most difficult tasks was not wasting too much time with issues that were not relevant to the specifics of the armed robbery. At times, it was difficult to not get caught up in the tips that would randomly come into the office.

I received an anonymous tip about a subject named Kevin Mikellvell attempting to contact both Alexander and McClinton. The report was that Mikellvell was trying to get Alexander and McClinton to change their story about what happened while he covertly recorded them. It was also part of the tip that Mikellvell was a client of Lucherini (Stewart's attorney). Among all of the tips that came into the robbery office about this case, this one caught my attention because it was connected to Lucherini.

Lucherini had tried to covertly record Eddie and me when we arrested Stewart at his office and it stood to reason his client would benefit if recordings appeared with Alexander and McClinton changing their stories about why they brought guns or that they didn't have guns. I contacted McClinton's attorney and set up a meeting with them. The next day, I sat down with McClinton and his attorney, Bill Terry, and asked about Mikellvell. McClinton did know Mikellvell and had a recent conversation him. When I told him about the tip I had received and what the tip alleged Mikellvell was doing, I could see McClinton processing through what I was saying. His physical reaction said more than anything that could have come out of his mouth. He was visibly angry. He and Terry assured me it did not matter who recorded McClinton. The truth was the truth and if anyone recorded McClinton, it would just be the same explanation of events just to a different person.

I tried to contact Alexander's attorney, but he never returned my call, so I contacted Alexander directly. I spoke with Alexander by phone and got a similar response as McClinton's. Alexander did know Mikellvell and had a recent conversation with him, but he claimed they did not talk about the case. Alexander did get profane when I explained how the tip claimed Mikellvell was attempting to get them to talk about the case while he recorded them. It was like he was recalling his conversation with Mikellvell and piecing together how Mikellvell was doing exactly what the tip alleged. Alexander also gave me reassurance of saying what happened in the hotel room was what happened and no one could change that.

I did not contact Lucherini, partly because I did not want to hear him lie to me through indirect lawyer double talk and partly because I was not concerned with the witness statements or the facts of the case. It was clear from both Alexander's and McClinton's reactions that Mikellvell was reaching out to them about the case, but facts are facts and as inconvenient as the facts were for Lucherini, they were not changing. I did find some comfort in Lucherini wasting his time coming up with this scheme that went nowhere.

Another tip that came into the office was from an inmate from one of the Nevada state prisons. The individual claimed to have information about Simpson trying to set up people in the past to take property back from them, too. Dealing with inmates is always a crapshoot; most have an underlying motive and will tell officers and detectives what they think they want to hear so they can achieve their own goal. If the information an inmate is providing has value, then I will try to figure out a motive. If there is no value in what they have told me, then I don't care what the motive was. They can just go back to their cell and work on the next idea for attention. The prison was only an hour's drive away from Las Vegas, so Eddie and I headed up to see what this inmate was claiming he knew about things Simpson had done in the past in regard to setting other people up.

We interviewed the inmate in a large room used for visitation at the prison. The room was empty other than the inmate, a couple of guards who were standing off at a distance, Eddie and me. After a short time of talking with this guy, it was clear he was just wasting our time. He had nothing to offer. I was polite and listened to him for a few minutes, then thanked him for his time and waved the guards over to us, ending the conversation.

Other tips occasionally came into the office, but most had nothing to do with the robbery. I read through every tip, even if it was garbage, because it was important to me to make sure I had all the pertinent information about the case that was out there. Part of the problem, though, was some of the tips were better suited for the *National Enquirer* than the police department.

While I did not enjoy all of the news coverage, I was genuinely entertained by most of the satire being pumped out faster than I could have ever imagined. It seemed like I could not turn on the TV or radio without hearing some comical reference to O.J. Simpson. One of my favorite moments was when O.J. Simpson's attorney, Yale Galanter, held a press conference on the steps of the Regional Justice Center during one of Simpson's court dates. A man wearing an "O.J. 07" shirt was able to make his way to a position just behind Galanter. The man was Jake Byrd, a comedian often seen on the "Jimmy Kimmel Live" late-night TV show. He was wearing a nerdy baseball hat, wire-framed glasses and had a large gap in his teeth, which was visible because of his ridiculous smile. As reporters asked Galanter questions, Byrd would yell goofy responses mocking the whole situation. A reporter asked an odd question, "Is your client innocent or not guilty?" Galanter, surrounded by a large crowd and standing behind microphones from both local and national media outlets, responded by saying, "I'm not sure there is a difference in the eyes of the law." Byrd immediately followed up by emphatically yelling and waving his hands, "He's both, dude. He's innocent and not guilty. Thank you." As Galanter continued to answer questions, Byrd stood behind him nodding and smiling in support. Byrd would point to Galanter and act like he was cheering him on; he even attempted to get high fives from Galanter for some of Galanter's answers. All the while, Byrd was awkwardly smiling and randomly sticking his tongue out. It was funny to watch.

Among the satire, there was also the occasional interview given by people involved in the case. I received a call from Roger, asking me to review any interview I could find given by anyone involved in the case. He wanted to know if the victims or witnesses ever gave different versions of what happened the night of the robbery. He initially asked me to contact media outlets in which various interviews had been given and request transcripts of the interviews. This seemed like it would be an easy task until I found that the people involved in the case had given close to 50 interviews and to get one transcript it took a few hours. At that time, Eddie and I were back to working our normal caseload, too, receiving about 20 new robbery cases a month. Neither of us had time to haggle with each of the media outlets for transcripts of the interviews. I called Roger back and made a compromise: we would review every interview we could find on the medium it was originally broadcast and if there was a substantive change in someone's story, I would then go through the process of getting the transcript. This seemed to work for Roger and, luckily for me, I never found a change of detail in any essential area of the investigation.

About two weeks after the preliminary hearing, Eddie and I were in Owens' office. He was happy with the transcription from the six minutes of the robbery, but he made it clear he felt like we needed to spend more time on the rest of Riccio's recordings. I told him we would start on them in our down time, which seemed to catch him a little off guard. He did not know Eddie and I were back to working our normal caseload. He called Roger, who also did not know we were working other cases. Roger called over to our office and requested Eddie and I be allowed to be dedicated to the Simpson case for approximately one to two months. Let there be no mistake, this was a nice relief for Eddie and me, but we knew when we got back to the office we were in for some healthy ball-busting from the other detectives in the robbery section.

After reviewing the case file with Owens, Eddie and I headed back to the robbery office. The robbery section was made up of four squads of six to eight detectives per squad. It was one of the more elite units and it was generally staffed with the more talented detectives from our department. As a general rule, I have found the more talented the officer or detective is, the more aggressive they are in their personality, too. This means not everyone gets along all the time and not everyone is the best of friends. Because of that dynamic, there is an odd twist that might seem like bullying outside of an office full of aggressive personalities, but inside the walls of the robbery office, you had better have thick skin and if you don't, you might need to find a different unit to work in. In fact, the dynamic created in this kind of environment can be quite backwards: if you are not well liked, you are just ignored, so there was almost a feeling of belonging when the hazing or ball-busting happened. Without question, the detectives who are friends are harder on each other than anyone else.

As I walked into the office, I knew I was about to get hit pretty hard for not having to take on new cases for a while.

Det. Scott Kavon was the first person who saw me. He was typing at his desk and stopped as I got closer. "Well, well, well, who do we have here? It's the superstars. They're too good to work like the rest of us."

Det. Mark Gregory, who was not normally prone to hazing, jumped in and told me, "Don't worry about real police work. We'll take care of that for you." That came from the few day shift guys. When our squad came, it was laid on much thicker. But if I were on the other side of the coin, I would have been dishing it out pretty hard, too, so I readily accepted the truth that sometimes you're the windshield and sometimes you're the bug.

Eddie and I went back to the transcription room at our office, where we sat sometimes for the entire week just listening and re-listening. At first, the edits were easy, but after a month, we were only adding a word here and there for every few minutes of audio. It got to the point where I could start quoting the various people on the recordings.

We were not just working on the recordings from Riccio. We also had little odds and ends come up here and there that needed to be taken care of. And, truth be told, I would jump at the smallest of reasons to get away from the recordings after the first couple of weeks.

By January 2008, we had a pretty good handle on the transcriptions. Owens always wanted them a little better, but at some point, Eddie and I are both cops and there was only so much transcribing we could do when we saw our coworkers out handling cases and arresting bad guys.

On Jan. 3, Roger called me in the morning and asked if I could come down to his office and interview Miguel Pereira later that afternoon. Pereira was the owner of You Ring We Spring Bail Bonds, which provided the bail bond for O.J. Simpson. I headed down to the DA's Office and met with Pereira, who had growing concerns about Simpson being out on a bond he wrote. Pereira expressed his concerns of Simpson violating the terms of his bail set by Judge

Bonaventure and he was also concerned because he was told by an anonymous source of O.J. Simpson's plans to go to Cuba to avoid the trial. If this happened, Pereira would lose the $125,000 bond that was posted for Simpson's release.

In Nevada, the bail bond industry is regulated and to secure the bond, a person has to pay the bail bond company 15 percent of the total bond. In this case, Simpson or someone for Simpson had to pay Pereira $18,750. Pereira puts up a bond for $125,000 and keeps the $18,750 no matter what happens. It is a highly profitable business, as long as the subject who is out on bail shows up for court. If not, then the losses get pretty big. Pereira played a voicemail left on Nov. 16, 2007, which was causing him concern:

"Hey Miguel, it's me _____ I just want, want C.J. to know that the whole thing all the time he was tellin' me that shit, ya know, I hope he was telling me the truth. Don't be trying to change the motherfucking shit now, motherfucking assholes. I'm tired of this shit. Fed up with motherfuckers changing what they told me. All right?"

Pereira wasn't too concerned by the voicemail itself. He also received an anonymous call from a male with a blocked phone number who told Pereira about Simpson taking a large private boat to the Bahamas. If this were true, Pereira was concerned Simpson could go to Cuba and Pereira would lose his money. Pereira told me of his intent to arrest O.J. Simpson and bring him back to the Clark County Detention Center so he could have his $125,000 bond returned.

At 5 a.m. on Jan. 11, 2008, I received a call from Pereira, who was in Florida about to make contact with O.J. Simpson to arrest him. Pereira asked me if I could call the local police department in Florida to let them know he was about to arrest Simpson. That is normally something I would not get involved in; the agreement between a bail agent and the person out on bail is not a police matter. A bail agent's ability to arrest an individual they have bonded is governed by state law and is consented to by the person they are providing the bail for. Simpson was aware of Pereira's right to bring him back to the Clark County Detention Center at any time based on a standard agreement when any subject is bail bonded out of jail. Though this is something I would normally stay away from, I knew this could create a problem for the local police department in Florida. I could see Simpson or people around Simpson calling the police and reporting a confrontation between Pereira and Simpson.

I called the Miami Police Department and spoke with Sgt. Ankeny, a supervisor in the area where Pereira was planning on arresting Simpson. I gave Sgt. Ankeny the details I had and provided him with Pereira's contact information. Pereira called me after he had Simpson in custody, informed me he was recording their entire contact and they would be traveling back to Las Vegas on a commercial flight. I contacted Sgt. Ken Seifert at the Las Vegas airport to let him know Simpson was going to be coming in on a flight from Florida in handcuffs and would be walking through the airport later that day. Sgt. Seifert asked for Pereira's contact information so he could plan for any security concerns that might arise.

Sgt. Seifert was not going to be at work when Simpson and Pereira arrived in Las Vegas, so he passed on the information to Sgt. Pete Rossi, who helped me make the arrangements to arrest Alexander at the airport back in September. Pete made preparations for Simpson to not have to walk through the crowds at the terminal. Pete and a couple of officers who work for him met Simpson and Pereira as they left the airplane. They were escorted to an unmarked vehicle waiting to transport them to Pereira's vehicle.

As friends, Pete and I had a moment to laugh about the strange feeling of contacting O.J. Simpson. Pete experienced that momentary strange paradox when Simpson's fame clashes with the reports of his criminal actions. It is an odd moment the both of us agreed we could never forget. Pete was able to get Pereira and Simpson to Pereira's vehicle without any incidents or media contact. When Pereira arrived at the Clark County Detention Center, it happened to be one of the days MyNetwork TV's "Jail" show was being filmed and Simpson's entire rebooking process was filmed. When he was finally taken to his room, he was assigned to Room 32. The officers who walked him to his room couldn't help but point out the irony of him being placed in Room 32, which was his uniform number in college and in the NFL.

Simpson would only stay in the Clark County Detention Center for a few days before he had a hearing in front of Judge Jackie Glass, who would be the trial judge. She gave him further admonishments about the conditions of his bail and raised his bail to $250,000. Simpson's bail was posted as soon as he was eligible and he got on a plane back to Florida.

Pereira would later provide me with the audio recordings from his contact with Simpson, but they didn't have any value to the armed robbery investigation. He also informed me that Scotto, O.J. Simpson's friend, called him after he arrested Simpson and threatened him. Pereira reported Scotto said, "I know where you live and I'm going to take care of you." Pereira also reported receiving harassing calls from Christie Prody after arresting Simpson. I advised Pereira that he needed to contact the local police where Prody and Scotto lived to report their harassing behavior. When I heard this, I could not help but to be brought back to this recurring thought of how Simpson had fallen from being surrounded by friends like Robert Kardashian to surrounding himself with thugs who make threats of violence when things don't go their way.

On the same day Pereira was arresting Simpson, I received a call from Beardsley, who had just been released from prison in California for violating his parole by being in Las Vegas without having permission from his parole officer. He wanted to know if I could get his property back that was taken when he was arrested. Doing the legwork to get property back for someone who was arrested would be strictly a courtesy on my end. It is definitely something I would not normally do, but I had never had one of my victims arrested before.

I agreed to get his property for him and he told me he was going to be at the Luxor Hotel and Casino the next day to pick up all the property from his hotel room that was left behind when he was arrested right after the armed robbery. The hotels normally collect all the belongings of a person who disappears and keeps them in a safe place for a reasonable amount of time or until the owner returns. Beardsley had already been in contact with the Luxor, so I did not need to do anything for him on that end. I met with Beardsley and gave him back his property. He gave me an earful about how much he hated Riccio and how he felt like the audio recordings had been edited. He told me how much he did not like the district attorney and how he did not feel he was being treated fairly because he does not want to be a victim in this case anymore. I tried to remember he had just gotten out of prison and was probably frustrated that he did not get the attention from me or the media that he wanted. My empathy for Beardsley only went so far because I felt like he was trying to work an angle, somehow thinking if he said he no longer wanted to be a victim that the case would all go away. This was quite the different tune than what he is heard ranting on Riccio's recording after the robbery; at that time, he was intent on making sure Simpson was held accountable for robbing him and Fromong.

I felt like Beardsley had been talking with people who had convinced him to back out of being a victim. Beardsley was not changing his story as to what happened; he now simply thought everyone should just forget about it and move on. As politely as I could under those circumstances, I explained to Beardsley that while he was a victim, his part of being a victim was very minimal in the big picture; it was Fromong who took the biggest loss and who was physically hurt as a result of the robbery. Beardsley would not admit to being contacted by anyone who tried to convince him to drop the charges, but it was clear to me something along those lines had happened. Beardsley and I did not part on the best of terms.

This feeling of someone trying to persuade Beardsley out of being a victim caused me to go through Beardsley's phone records to see if there was anything out of the ordinary. There were only a few days of records to review because Beardsley was arrested for his parole violation shortly after the robbery. I did notice a pattern that was concerning, but only after looking at Simpson's and Beardsley's records together. Both Beardsley and Simpson were calling and receiving calls from a number I did not recognize and these calls were all in close proximity to each other. There were 19 calls in two days involving Beardsley, Simpson and an unidentified number. I was able to determine the unknown number belonged to Associated Press reporter Linda Deutsch. It is possible Deutsch was simply gathering as much information as she could for an AP report.

I also reviewed the phone calls Simpson made when he was in jail immediately after he was arrested. The first call that caught my attention was a call Simpson made to his daughter Arnelle. In order to receive a call from an inmate from the Clark County Detention Center, a person must set up an account with the phone system the jail uses. It basically ensures the receiver of the call knows calls from the jail are collect calls and are recorded. The inmate can call a number without an account having been setup, but when the call is connected, a recording plays that both parties can hear: "We're sorry, but the person you called does not have an account. We will try to help them set up." Right before the recording plays, the inmate has a second or two to say something that can also be heard by the person the inmate called. During this call, O.J. Simpson was able to get out, "Uh, I hope it doesn't hang up. Uh … you have, uh, have Arnelle call Beardsley. Want a—." Then the recording played and the phone system hung up.

Another call Simpson made shortly after he was arrested was interesting for investigative purposes because it was revealing about his character. Simpson called an unidentified female and told her, "OK. Um. Uh. Hey, tell Tommy then everybody needs to watch whatever they are talkin' about on the phone because these guys. You know. I said I, they, they tell ya they're listening to my call now. Just say, tell everybody to watch what they say on any of their phones. 'Cause [inaudible] even, even if they weren't even with me, I bet ya everybody's phone is bugged for whatever reason. Ya know." If you are being honest and not trying to manipulate the truth, then you don't have to worry about what people say even if they are recorded. This simple recorded statement spoke volumes about Simpson and the people he was associating with.

These connections were not a big concern because Beardsley was not changing the facts; he just no longer wanted to be a victim who wanted Simpson to be prosecuted for what he did to him. Though it was not a big concern, it was interesting to see the lengths Simpson would go to earn back Beardsley's good favor.

A week later, I was contacted by Pereira, who wanted to give me two books that he reported were given to him by Simpson's attorney, Galanter. Pereira alleged Galanter gave him the books during the preliminary hearing. He described the books to me and they sounded like the ones I recovered when I arrested Stewart, but Fromong had never mentioned books being stolen.

The next day, I contacted Fromong and asked him if he could come down to my office to view the property that I recovered when Cashmore and Stewart turned themselves in to be arrested. As he looked through the photos taken of the recovered property, he believed there were at least 200 missing autographed pictures. He instantly recognized the books "I Want To Tell You" as being stolen and explained he had forgotten he brought them to the room. When I told him there were 18 recovered, he was quick to tell me there should have been 20 books in the box. He believed all the plaques and footballs he had stolen from him were in the pictures I showed him. He also expressed concerns for his Pete Rose autographed baseballs and a pair of Duke Snyder turf-worn shoes that were also taken during the armed robbery but not recovered when Cashmore or Stewart were arrested. Unfortunately, I was never able to locate those last items that were stolen from Fromong, but when he confirmed there were two missing books, I knew the books Pereira had called me about were part of Fromong's stolen property. Before Fromong left the Robbery Office, he also told me about Beardsley contacting him and asking him to drop the charges.

On Jan. 23, 2008, Eddie and I went to Pereira's business, where he gave me the two books. Pereira explained how on the morning Cashmore was going to testify in the preliminary hearing, he drove Simpson to attorney Gabe Grasso's office; Grasso was Simpson's local attorney who was assisting Galanter. When they got there, he said Grasso took Simpson into the conference room and Galanter stopped Pereira. Miguel claimed Galanter handed him the two books and told him that they were intended for a back-up plan to discredit Cashmore by claiming Cashmore was trying to secure bail with the books before he was arrested. I could not piece together how or why this would discredit Cashmore, so I did not put too much stock in this explanation. There was no doubt in my mind something was going on as to why Pereira was given the books, but I feared it could easily become a distraction to the simple facts of the case. This was exactly the kind of bunny trail I did not want to follow; it sounds juicy, but it did not change what happened in the room and I wanted to be vigilant about not creating talking points for the defense to distract the jury during the upcoming trial.

I had one last recording to work on that contained

important statements that help to understand Simpson's mindset after the robbery. It was the conversation McClinton recorded at the party after the armed robbery in a restaurant called Little Buddha in the Palms Resort and Casino. I had sent the microcassette tape of the recording made by McClinton to the FBI to have the quality enhanced. When the enhanced recording returned from the FBI, I started transcribing its contents. McClinton reported in his statement that Simpson had said something about guns, but he couldn't remember exactly what it was and he noted they were in a loud restaurant, so everything was hard to hear on the tape. The enhanced version was remarkably better. Simpson, Alexander, McClinton and a group of unidentified individuals were talking for about five minutes about the robbery they had just committed. They were focused on how the property belonged to Simpson, so it should not be a big deal. As they talked, it sounds like they are trying to convince themselves it was no big deal. Then the conversation shifted to the police and what we were probably doing. The group talked about how we were probably talking to the victims and watching the surveillance video, then Simpson says:

**Simpson:**... [Inaudible] a lotta stuff [inaudible] It doesn't matter, they got [inaudible] they gonna, they gonna look at the, the video.

**Unknown:**Look, but even in the video ...

**Simpson:**You didn't pull the piece out in the hall.

**McClinton:**No, no, no, no, no, no, hell no.

**Simpson:**There ain't nothin' on that video and look, they gonna look at the video. They're probably gonna look at that video. They gonna get all the video. Look at it before they decide what they gonna do. Ain't nothin' they can see. They gonna see us goin' in the place. Then they gonna see us leaving with just the boxes.

As I listened to the enhanced audio, the statement Simpson made was clear and the context was undeniable. Simpson was not asking a question. He was telling the group, "You didn't pull the piece out in the hall." He was building everyone's confidence that it was going to be their word against the victims'. It was clear he knew there was going to be video showing them coming and going, but he did not think there was video of the guns. There was some more inaudible conversation where everyone was talking over each other and then McClinton says something that sounds like it is in response to a question, "No, I kept that thing in my pocket till we got inside that room." Though the conversation is inaudible, it is clear in context he was asked by someone there who wanted to verify McClinton did not have his gun out in the hallway before they went into the room. It was Simpson who was leading the conversation, but I was not able to definitively say McClinton was responding to a question by Simpson; it is, however, what makes sense when the totality of the conversation is taken into account. In the recording, when Simpson is talking about the property they stole, Simpson is also heard saying, "And I knew, to be honest with you. I knew now the Goldmans would get it and sell it and so I, I told these guys do whatever you wanna do with it."

McClinton's recording not only provided evidence of Simpson's knowledge of guns being used, it also pointed toward his desire to take extreme measures to avoid paying his court-ordered debts.

As I finished up working through all the audio recordings I had to work with, I needed to turn my attention to the phone records of everyone involved. I had obtained the phone records of everyone involved in the armed robbery through grand jury subpoenas. The phone records helped to confirm the statements of the subjects who had decided to be honest and accept responsibility for their involvement and they also helped me to establish the times on Riccio's recordings. There were times on the various recordings when phone calls were made or received and I was able to match those calls to phone records to establish the times when the recordings were made. The phone records showed how all the suspects were talking with each other throughout the evening, but it would take hours to go through them and explain them to a jury, which was a problem. I began working on a chart to provide a visual explanation of the phone records.

After I had the basic idea of the chart laid out, I contacted an analyst on our department, Dawn Leslie, who specialized in making large visual aids. She was able to put together a chart that was about three feet tall and about four feet long, containing all of the phone records from all of the suspects on the evening of the armed robbery. It takes a few moments to acclimate to the layout of the chart, but within minutes, any person could look at the chart and see there was a substantial amount of contact before and after the robbery.

Dawn also worked on a timeline chart that was similar in size. The timeline started with the planning at the pool area in the Palms Resort and Casino and went through to the suspects leaving the Palace Station after the robbery. When I picked up the finished timeline, Dawn told me how she did not list O.J. Simpson as the first suspect, but she did assign the color red to Simpson on the timeline because she felt red drew attention to him. The timeline included pictures and factual notes that I provided based on the investigation. The combination of the phone chart and timeline painted a self-explanatory picture of the planning and execution of the armed robbery.

By the time March 2008 came rolling around, Eddie and I had most of the work done on the case. But March also brought with it the new trial date of September.

The last big curveball thrown my way during the investigation was Riccio writing a book before the trial. By the end of February, Eddie and I were back to our normal cases and I wasn't focused on the Simpson case. In July 2008, I received a call from Roger, who asked me to come down to his office. When I got there, he handed me a copy of "Busted!" by Thomas Riccio. The front of the book had a picture of Riccio next to the Las Vegas booking photo of O.J. Simpson. David handed me the book and asked me to read it to verify there were no new revelations or changes that he needed to know about. I took the book home and started reading. There is nothing like reading a book you don't want to read. The book is more of an autobiography than it was about the robbery in Las Vegas. In fact, there are only a few pages dedicated to the events that surrounded the robbery. His cover is misleading. If you were to see it in the store, you would think Riccio was arrested, too, and the book was all about the armed robbery in Las Vegas.

I called Roger back a few days later to tell him there was nothing in the book that I could see having any effect on the case. I'm pretty sure Roger had already read the book, but because I would be the one testifying on the stand, he wanted me to know what was in the book in case the defense asked me about it.

By the end of August, I was back to meeting with Owens on a regular basis to review the case for the trial coming up the next month. There was no new information to go over and the investigation had been mostly done for months, but there were more than 1,000 pages of statements, reports and transcribed recordings to review. In the few months that had passed, I had already started to forget where important facts were located, but by the time jury selection started, I was back up to speed and ready to testify in what would be one of the most followed cases in Las Vegas history.

# CHAPTER 15
# THE TRIAL

The last hurdle for me before the trial started was Beardsley. He had been arrested again for another parole violation and was in prison. He was transported to the Clark County Detention Center and held there during the trial. When he arrived, he told Roger he was not willing to testify. Roger called me and asked me if I could go down to the jail to talk with him to see what was wrong. I told Roger that Beardsley and I did not have the most friendly of a contact the last time we were around each other and I thought it would be better if Linda talked with him. Roger agreed that would probably work out better.

Linda went down to the jail and met with Beardsley. Linda was able to identify one of Beardsley's biggest issues: he was worried about how he looked. Beardsley had been in prison for a while. His hair and nails were not in the condition he liked and he did not want to be seen like that. Linda worked with the jail staff to arrange for his hair and nails to be cut. Linda perfectly identified that Beardsley was self-absorbed and he liked attention; she knew if he were happy with how he looked, there would not be a chance he would pass on testifying in a trial involving O.J. Simpson. He still did not like Roger, believed Riccio had edited the recordings and thought I was a dirty cop—even saying I wore a "clean shirt but dirty underwear"—but he was still going to testify.

There was this role reversal in the couple of weeks leading up to the trial. There were times over the last year when my life was completely consumed with this investigation and now, I was seeing that total consumption in both Roger and Owens. Roger and Owens extended me the courtesy of involving me in their courtroom strategy, but the reality was

I did not have enough experience to know the inner workings of a jury trial. In an abundance of caution of the possibility that Judge Glass was not going to allow the jury to take a trip to the Palace Station to see Room 1203, Roger had a replica of the room built on an empty floor in the Regional Justice Center. Roger and Owens also had sessions with a jury consultant, which they let me sit in on. The ideas offered by the consultant made sense and it was interesting to listen to him but because I didn't, and still don't, fully understand courtroom tactics, I probably would have undervalued the importance and difficulty of picking an unbiased jury. It fascinated me to listen to them talk about how they were not looking for people to convict Simpson; rather, they were simply looking for people who were going to be fair and follow the law.

As I listened to them discuss the questionnaire all of the potential jurors were going to have to fill out, their concern for fairness was clear. The questionnaire asked questions about being a sports fan, about being a USC fan, about being a Buffalo Bills fan and about being an O.J. Simpson fan. The questionnaire also asked:

(94) Are you aware that O.J. Simpson was tried on criminal charges in California in a case unrelated to the case?

If yes, do you know the outcome of the California criminal case?

If yes, did you agree with the verdict in that trial?

What are your thoughts, feelings, or opinions, if any, about the criminal case?

Would you be able to set aside your feelings about that case and judge the charges against O.J. Simpson in this case based solely on the evidence presented during this trial and the instructions the Court gives the jurors?

(95)Are you aware that O.J. Simpson was sued in a civil court in California in a case that is unrelated to this case?

If yes, do you know the outcome of the California civil case?

If yes, did you agree with the verdict in that trial?

What are your thoughts, feelings, or opinions, if any, about the civil case?

Would you be able to set aside your feelings about that case and judge the charges against O.J. Simpson in this case based solely on the evidence presented during this trial and the instructions the Court gives the jurors?

(96)Are you aware that O.J. Simpson wrote a book titled, "If I Did It?"

If yes, have you read this book?

If yes, what are your thoughts, feelings, or opinions, if any, about it?

Can you set aside any opinions you may have developed as a result of reading the book and decide this case solely on the basis of evidence produced in court and the instructions on the law that the judge gives you?

There were a total of 116 questions and many of those had follow-up questions, all designed to identify individuals who would give O.J. Simpson a fair trial.

As Roger and Owens moved into the actual jury selection, I was essentially moved out of the process and put into a position of just waiting for the selection to be complete and the trial to start. Owens explained to me how he wanted to minimize the amount of officers and detectives he had to call. His preference was to only have Officer Chris Tucker, who was the initial responding officer, and myself testify. Though he had subpoenaed everyone else involved in the case, he felt I had the ability to best explain every aspect of the investigation. If he were able to limit detectives who only played a small role, he reduced the potential of a detective answering a question during the trial out of context. This meant I needed to review the thousands of pages of reports and transcriptions I had compiled by the start of the trial.

During my review, I attempted to gather seven or eight hundred pages of the most important documents and put them in a separate five-inch, three-ring binder that I could bring to the witness stand to reference as I testified. By the time the trial started, I felt like I knew most of the case by memory and the things that were not possible to memorize I had filed in a system I could quickly find in the binder I carried throughout the trial.

While jury selection was going on, I received a subpoena from Lucherini to be a defense witness in the upcoming trial against O.J. Simpson and Stewart. I had never been served a subpoena by a defense attorney to testify in a criminal trial for the defense. I asked around my office to see if anyone else had experienced the defense serving an officer or detective with a subpoena and no one had even heard of that happening. I called Owens to ask him why I was served by the defense. Owens asked which attorney subpoenaed me and I told him it was Lucherini. There is always an assumption of detectives knowing the rules of the courts, which is not universally true.

At that time, I did not understand the difference between what I could be asked as a prosecution witness and what I could be asked as a defense witness. Owens took a few moments to explain the limits on a defense attorney's questions to a prosecution witness revolve around what the prosecution asks. If I were a prosecution witness and the prosecution never asked me about the search warrants, then the defense would not get to ask me about them, either.

In general, the defense only gets to ask about the topics covered by the prosecution when it is a prosecution witness. By Lucherini serving a subpoena to be a defense witness, he circumvented that rule and the defense would now have opportunity to ask whatever they wanted.

The jury selection process took a week and ended with 12 jurors and six alternates. With the jurors selected, the trial was set to begin.

The trial began on Monday, Sept. 15, 2008, almost one year after the armed robbery occurred. Though I was not scheduled to testify until Wednesday, Owens had asked me to be available at court in case they needed something. As a witness, I was not permitted to watch or follow the testimony in the trial, so I brought a computer down to the courthouse to work on other cases while I waited.

The media frenzy from the preliminary hearing was not present at the start of the trial on that Monday morning. All of the major networks and cable news organizations were there, but the reporters and camera crews were not set up outside the court. In fact, other than the news trucks and vans consuming much of the normal public parking area, their presence could easily go unnoticed. I arrived at the courthouse a little early that morning to beat the morning rush. I never had a trial with Judge Glass and I wanted to get acclimated to the location of the courtroom and see if a bailiff was available to let me look in the courtroom to see what to expect.

Judge Glass's courtroom was on the south end of the hall. As I exited the elevator and rounded the corner toward her courtroom, I noticed there was an out-of-place table with a cardboard box on it outside of the entrance to her court. As I got closer, I could see someone had used a black marker to write "Cell Phones" on the box. The door from the main hallway into the foyer was unlocked, which was highly unusual for 8 a.m. I opened the door and a bailiff was standing there who instantly told me the courtroom was closed and I would have to wait outside. I was wearing a suit, so my badge and gun could not be seen underneath my jacket. There was no reason for the bailiff to think I was anything more than a lookie-loo. I always wore my gun and badge on my right side, so I pulled back my jacket just enough to show my badge and identified myself as a detective. I explained to him that I just wanted to see the courtroom to see what kind of media presence there would be and where their equipment would be set up. The doors into the court from the foyer were propped open and he waved me in. There were a few men in the back corner setting up camera equipment and running cables. The bailiff told me the back corner of the room was the only area the camera crews were going to be set up and somehow, all the media outlets were going to be all connected through that one camera crew. I didn't understand how that would all work and I really didn't care. I was primarily concerned with finding out if there were going to be cables all over the floor in areas I would have to walk. At the preliminary hearing, I was worried about tripping on national TV because of the cables running on the floor in the walkways. The cables were not an issue and after taking a moment to familiarize myself to the room, I asked the bailiff what the deal was with the table and box in the hallway. He told me Judge Glass said there would be no cell phones allowed in the court except for court staff, lawyers and officers.

As the trial began, the defense made an emotional argument that the property that was taken was not just memorabilia, but it was Simpson's personal property. When opening statements were completed, the prosecution called Fromong as its first witness. After a few hours on the witness stand, Fromong started feeling lightheaded and dizzy. Paramedics were called and Fromong was checked out, but he refused to be transported to the hospital. Due to Fromong already having a heart attack related to him being robbed, the court agreed it would not be a good idea to have him continue testifying that day. Fromong was the primary victim and the one who had to explain what happened in Room 1203 at the Palace Station on the night of Sept. 13, 2007. He had to describe why he was there, who was there and what happened before, during and after the robbery. He had to describe his loss, his fear and his hurt. He had to give details about how it changes your life to have a gun pointed at you in anger while someone takes property from you. After years of investigating robberies, I have seen how being robbed destroys people's ability to enjoy life without fear and I have seen it completely destroy a joyous person's outlook. Victims of robbery often struggle with being alone, being in dark places and they can suddenly start interacting differently with people who look like the person who robbed them. Those are all things I can describe that I have seen, but Fromong needed to explain it to the court.

The first day ended without any other remarkable incidents. The trial was moving along. In five years of working as a robbery detective, I had never experienced a robbery trial lasting more than two days. But for an armed robbery involving O.J. Simpson, two days was only going to scratch the surface of the information that was to be covered.

Day two brought witnesses and testimony about O.J. Simpson's civil lawsuit in which a jury found him liable for the deaths of Nicole Brown and Ron Goldman in the amount of $33.5 million. This was introduced to establish how even if 12 of the hundreds of items stolen from Fromong could have possibly been traced back to Simpson's ownership, then those 12 items would have been shown to have been unlawfully hidden to avoid paying his $33.5 million settlement. Simpson's defense had to try and deploy smoke and mirrors to distract the jury away from the simple facts of this crime. Ownership was not relevant, but even if the defense could get the jury to ignore the law and buy into the emotional argument of Simpson just getting back his property, that only applied to maybe 12 items out of hundreds which were stolen from Fromong.

Simpson's defense team did provide an opportunity for Stewart's defense to argue that Stewart could not have known the property was not Simpson's and therefore should be viewed as just helping a friend get his property back. But even for Stewart, that position could not work because of the Joe Montana and West Point memorabilia that was stolen also. He could have called the police immediately once he discovered he had been involved in taking another person's property and turned it in. But he didn't.

Sept. 17, 2008, was day three and it was going to be the first of what ended up being four times of me having to testify. Owens told me I was not going until the afternoon, so my nerves did not get to me too bad. Though there was a visible media presence, it did not feel intrusive like it did at the preliminary hearing. Judge Glass had created a more comfortable environment to work with under these circumstances. Owens told me I would start detailing the police response and an investigation overview and then he would see how much time there was to proceed into more specifics. In the morning, I just studied the case file I'd created with all the reports I thought I might need. I had time to study the file all morning, but as lunchtime approached, I was getting a little more nervous for all the same reasons that revolved around not wanting to embarrass myself or my police department.

I did not see Simpson in the hall on the first two days, but when the court broke for lunch on this day, I did see Simpson walk out of the courtroom. For a brief moment, he made eye contact with me from about 100 feet away. He smiled at me and gave me a wave. I responded with a head nod acknowledging his wave—how I would have normally responded to anyone else who smiled and waved at me. I looked away and after having a moment to think about it, I was mad at myself for even acknowledging him with a head nod. I should have just looked away. I can't think of a time when a robbery suspect I investigated ever smiled and waved at me. If it ever would have happened, I probably would have responded by confronting them and asking what their problem was.

My frustration grew as people who were fans surrounded him and treated him like he was better than the rest of us. I watched as he walked toward the elevators and the people in the hallway flocked to him. I waited for a few minutes after he left, then I headed to the elevators, too, so I could go to the cafeteria. When I got to the cafeteria, my frustration was compounded as I saw Simpson was there, too, and he was being treated like royalty; it would truly surprise me if someone did not pay for his meal. I ended up getting my food to go because I could not sit and watch people fawn over him. There was a nice byproduct of my frustration, which was it made me forget about my nerves and testifying in the next hour or so.

After lunch, court started back up and I waited in the witness room. As I sat there, I knew I was next and I was just waiting for the bailiff to come get me. He opened the door to the witness room and said they were ready for me. I grabbed my binder and headed into the courtroom for the witness stand. I had walked the same walk many times before and would walk it many times after the trial and there is always a nervous anticipation. Jury trials are considerably more in-depth than preliminary hearings, so they normally require more specificity and attention to detail. This time, it was amplified because of all the media attention being given to the trial.

As I remained standing, I placed my binder on the small desk of the witness stand. The judge's clerk asked me to raise my right hand and asked if I would swear the testimony I was about to give was the truth? "I do," I answered. I was then instructed to sit down and state my name for the record and spell my last name for the court reporter.

It is natural for me to survey the room once I have sat down and again, I got a big smile and this time also a head nod from O.J. I did not feel obligated to respond in this setting. Both Owens and Roger gave me head nods. Stewart did not make eye contact and I don't remember any of the defense attorneys looking up at me.

Owens was one of the most experienced prosecutors in the District Attorney's Office and I think he knew I was nervous, so he started by asking me simple questions about my employment and experience. Once Owens had established who I was and my background experience, he started asking open-ended questions about responding to the Palace Station in reference to a reported armed robbery. As I described my response and preliminary investigation, Owens asked if I could explain to the jury the court exhibit created to provide a timeline with pictures of the events of Sept. 13, 2007. Simpson's attorney objected and believed Simpson's line on the timeline was intentionally red to make him look more guilty. The objection was overruled and I was allowed to explain the exhibit.

The timeline started with the planning at the Palms and ended with O.J. Simpson and his friends walking out of the Palace Station with Fromong's property. Because Simpson was claiming there were no guns involved, I felt some of the pictures in the timeline were revealing about that fact. As O.J. Simpson and his friends entered the Palace Station, both McClinton and Alexander were wearing suits and their jackets were buttoned closed. As both McClinton and Alexander exited with Simpson, their jackets were unbuttoned, which would be necessary to access the guns they were carrying under their jackets. It was no smoking gun, but it added to the credibility of McClinton's and Alexander's testimony. I walked through every aspect of my investigation except the recordings.

After an hour or so, Owens turned me over to the defense. O.J. Simpson's attorney, Galanter, went first. He again covered my experience except his tone was patronizing and it felt like he was passively trying to establish his superiority over me. He asked if one of my responsibilities was to "marshal the evidence." I answered with a simple "Yes," and then, as if he caught me saying something wrong, he turned to the jury and asked if I understood what that meant and I again said, "Yes." He then asked me to explain what it meant to "marshal the evidence." I believe he was disappointed when I was able to give a reasonable explanation that marshaling the evidence included examining and taking orderly custody of the evidence. He had no curveball questions that I recognized and I tried to be polite and to answer the questions he asked in the way he asked them. He then passed me to Stewart's attorneys. Stewart's second attorney, Brent Bryson, handled questioning me. Bryson greeted me and only asked me a few questions. He asked me if Stewart turned himself in and I answered, "Yes." He followed up by asking me if Stewart voluntarily turned himself in and I answered, "Yes." He ended his cross-examination and reminded the court I was under subpoena by the defense as well, which they would want to further examine me at a later time. It was approaching 5 p.m. and the judge adjourned court for the day. I was to come back to be the first witness the next morning. I was feeling pretty good about my testimony.

When I was excused, I waited in the witness room to walk out with Owens and Roger. As Owens walked out of the court, he had a disappointed look on his face and asked me why I was so easy on the defense. He caught me off guard and I did not understand what he was talking about. We were alone in the hall and he started to give me some examples. He asked if Stewart voluntarily turned himself in and I said yes. Owens asked me if I served a search warrant on his house, if I had him identified and if his picture was on the news as one of the suspects in the robbery, which was all true. And then Owens said Stewart did not turn himself in voluntarily. I saw his point; I was so focused on answering as fast as I could that I was not thinking through the questions.

Owens continued to tell me I needed to disrupt the flow

of the defense attorneys by asking them to repeat themselves if they asked a long question and point out when they ask multiple questions in one question. Owens also told me I needed to try and cram in more than one-word answers if I could. If I could see the defense was trying to get in a half-truth, I needed to try and give the truth. The example that stuck out in my mind was when Galanter asked about a couple of the stolen items being addressed to O.J. Simpson. Rather than just saying "yes," there were some items addressed to Simpson I should respond with something along the lines of, "Mixed in with the West Point and Joe Montana stuff, there were a couple items addressed to Simpson." Owens' point was well taken and I knew I needed to work better on that for the next morning.

After the trial was over, I was given a courtesy copy of all my testimony. I took the opportunity to watch my first day of testifying and I did see many missed opportunities, but none more glaring than when Bryson asked me about Stewart voluntarily turning himself in. Bryson had a note pad full of questions at the podium where the attorneys often stood to ask witness questions. In the moment, I did not see Bryson testing me to see how fast I was answering my questions. When he asked me if Stewart turned himself in, I said, "Yes." I could see on the video his demeanor changed. He then asked if Stewart voluntarily turned himself in and when I said, "Yes," I could see on the video that the value of me saying Stewart voluntarily turned himself in was more important than any other response he could have gotten out of me. He reviewed his notes he brought up to the podium and then told the judge and jury he had no further questions for me at that time. In getting to watch the video after the fact, I could see how Bryson used my answer to create the impression of Stewart wanting to come forward because it was the right thing to do rather than turning himself in because he knew I was coming for him and he wanted to be arrested when it was convenient for himself. My response gave the defense the ability to make Stewart look like he was completely cooperative and even helpful.

Though the jury had not yet listened to Riccio's audio recordings, my testimony on Thursday was going to cover much of what I did with the recordings. On Wednesday night, I reviewed the transcripts I had worked on for so many hours. I had to process the directions Owens gave me to make sure the defense was not manipulating facts to minimize their client's guilt.

By the time I arrived at court on Thursday, I was feeling pretty comfortable. I had committed to myself to maintain a professional demeanor while trying to slow any momentum the defense was building and also ensure I was getting the whole truth out if the defense tried to solicit half-truths. As I took my seat at the witness stand, I had the awkward moment with Simpson again where he smiled at me and gave me a head nod. It was almost like he had a need to connect with me.

Owens started the day by asking me if Stewart voluntarily turned himself in. This time, I gave a more detailed answer by explaining the reality that he was forced by my actions to turn himself in. I was able to more correctly show how his actions being arrested were more selfish than honorable. He knew he was going to be arrested for his crimes, but he wanted to be arrested on his terms.

Owens then moved on to Riccio's recordings and how I transcribed them. He established my personal contact with all of the suspects, witnesses and victims, to illustrate my ability to identify who was talking on the recordings when I transcribed them. Owens played the six minutes of the robbery for the jury, which needed very little explanation. As he played the recording of the robbery, he had designed a way for the jury to watch the transcribed dialogue on monitors where the statements made were connected to the person who made the statement. Those six minutes of audio was damning evidence of a volatile encounter. Owens had me show the jury the guns used by Alexander and McClinton and had me tie in the small size of Room 1203 to illustrate the various factors that compounded Simpson's violent nature and his friends' actions as they stole Fromong's property. Owens then passed me to the defense.

Galanter gave me the obligatory greeting then began asking about Simpson's involvement. It was clear he was going down a path of trying to establish how others might have stolen property, but Simpson did not steal anything. Galanter asked me if Simpson had taken a wallet from the victims. Here is where I leaned on Owens' directions. While it was true Simpson did not take the victim's wallet, he did violently grab the phone out of Fromong's hand. Galanter was trying to play on a public perception of "robbery" and distract from the actual crime of robbery being taking any property from another person by force or fear of force. I politely responded to Galanter's question by saying, "I believe Mr. Simpson only grabbed Mr. Fromong's phone out of his hand." Galanter was quick to tell me that is not what he asked, which I knew, but I also knew he did not want the jury to consider the full truth. He again asked a similar question about Simpson taking Fromong's watch, which did not happen, but he was again clearly trying to point to a traditional understanding of a robber pointing a gun at a victim and demanding a watch or wallet. I politely gave the same response. I could see Galanter getting frustrated with me and asked the judge to instruct me to just answer the question. Judge Glass asked me to just answer the question with a yes or no. Galanter went for a third try at a similar question and I gave a similar response. The third time, his frustration grew to him telling me I knew I was not to answer the way I was answering. Judge Glass admonished me again and Galanter moved on in a different direction.

Galanter's assertion that I knew better was not true. I had no extensive training in testifying in court and I don't know all the rules of the court, but I did trust Owens and I knew it was best to get the whole truth out even if the defense did not like it. When Galanter would ask complex questions, I would ask him to repeat the question and if his question were incomplete—even if I knew where he was going—I would still ask him to repeat the question. Galanter was visibly unhappy with me and passed me to Stewart's team.

While Lucherini was asking me questions about Stewart's actions before the robbery, he had used the wrong name of someone Stewart had contact with. I knew exactly what he was talking about and I could have easily corrected him and given him the answer he was looking for. But there is a reality in his mistake; his mistake made what he was asking untrue and if I were so unprepared and used the wrong name in my testimony, he would pounce on me as being incompetent and unfit to conduct an investigation like this. When he asked about the contact between Stewart and the wrong name he was using, I answered by telling him I did not know the person he was talking about. After Lucherini checked his notes, he got the name right and I affirmed his question. It was not my job to get the jury to acquit Simpson and Stewart. I knew they were guilty and I was there to ensure I represented the truth.

My time on the stand went well with the exception of how I responded to the defense attorneys on the first day. There were limited high points once the details of the robbery were spelled out and the audio of the robbery was played. When it came to the recordings, there were a couple funny moments that were a little uncomfortable for me. When it came time for jurors to listen to the various audio recordings, they were given some instructions by Judge Glass:

"Now, ladies and gentlemen of the jury, before we commence playing of the tape, let me advise you that the tape recordings are received into evidence. The transcripts you have been given have been prepared by the State of Nevada for use as an aid while listening to the tapes in court. The parties have not agreed as to the accuracy of the identities of the various speakers, or the contents of the transcripts. The tapes are the actual evidence in this case, and the transcripts are not evidence. If you perceive any variation between the contents of the tape, and the contents of the transcripts, or the identity of the speaker, you must be solely guided by the tapes or other evidence admitted in this case, and not the transcripts. Of course, if you don't want to use the transcripts, you are not required to do that, either. If you cannot determine from the tape that particular words are spoken, you must disregard the transcript insofar as those words are concerned."

It is important to note the FBI was able to definitively eliminate the possibility of any tampering with the audio recordings and the FBI analyst who worked on the recordings testified as to the extent of his review and enhancement of them. Regardless of how much Fromong and Beardsley did not like the contents of the recordings or their reasoning for believing they were not accurate, the recordings were accurate and factual.

The defense made a couple of attempts at challenging some of my transcriptions, but I could not concede their interpretations in those few places—not because they were challenging my work, but because I did not hear what they were suggesting. The couple of areas they questioned did not seem relevant to the charges or the actions, but I also understood they might have just been trying to plant seeds of the potential for errors in the transcripts in the minds of the jurors. The uncomfortable moments came as the defense asked me about some of the statements made by other law enforcement personnel who were recorded when they believed they were alone in Room 1203 after the robbery.

There were monitors in the courtroom set up for the jury to see and there was one set up in the witness stand. Simpson's defense team put a section of the transcript up and asked me to read it. I instantly recognized the statement because I had listened to the recordings and reviewed the transcripts ad nauseam. Eddie was talking to other law enforcement personnel while standing in Room 1203 when we did not know there was a recorder in the room. Eddie was telling the other personnel in the room about our disbelief when we had first arrived at the Palace Station and started interviewing Fromong, then he recounts in his own colorful way what he thought when he saw O.J. Simpson in the surveillance video at the time of the robbery. I looked at the statements and I did just as I was asked to do by the defense, I read: "LaNeve: And then even before, we started our interviews before we started lookin' at the video and we were like, this guy's full of shit." And, "LaNeve: You see him rollin' up like a fuckin' shitbag."

I had always maintained the disbelief Eddie and I had when we first met Fromong and Beardsley, so the defense was obviously highlighting the inflammatory nature of these comments. I don't believe it worked because jurors are people just like anyone else. They might not have been as profane in their delivery, but I would imagine they had similar thoughts when they found out they were going to be serving on O.J. Simpson's trial. I don't believe it was unusual for anyone to think there was no way Simpson would be involved in an armed robbery in a hotel room at the Palace Station and I don't think it was unusual to have an adverse reaction when we saw it really was him. I remember experiencing a moment of levity before I read Eddie's comments and the defense asked me what he meant by his statements. I told them I could not speak for Eddie. The defense had to know I was not able to testify about what Eddie was thinking when he made those statements.

They continued to ask about statements other people made, knowing I could not explain the statements, but I was the vessel they used to highlight comments made by others on the recordings. Mike Perkins was the criminalistics supervisor who was in Room 1203 after the robbery when Riccio's recorder was still recording. Mike was talking with Eddie about his initial thoughts before he responded to the Palace Station when he read that O.J. Simpson was one of the suspects. I believe the defense wanted to create an idea that we would do anything to "get him" because California couldn't. Eddie was talking about how it was a slow night before we responded to Palace Station and how we could not have prepared for this case.

> **LaNeve:** We were so slow. We went out to the 407 on, uh, right down Trop. It came out just prior to this one. Uhm, and we were cherry pickin'. We were gonna take it from Patrol. But it was a bullshit, date rape robbery, and you're not [inaudible].
>
> **Perkins:** Hey, it gives us somethin' to do.
>
> **LaNeve:** Yeah, we'll take. And uh, we were back, actually back at the office.
>
> **Perkins:** Then you got another one.
>
> **LaNeve:** Yeah. We had to drop that, give it back to Patrol. Come out, deal with this.
>
> **Perkins:** Man. Sorry, guys, but this one's a little bit [inaudible].
>
> **Unknown:** [Inaudible] all this [inaudible].
>
> **Perkins:** This is great. Yeah. Uh, John said, he's like, yeah. California can't get him [inaudible] now we'll be [inaudible] got him.

I again could not speak for someone else, so I simply read what they asked me to read and politely responded that they would need to ask Eddie and Mike if they wanted clarification. For all the defense's attempts to highlight off-color statements, it did not change the facts of the crimes committed.

From my limited perspective as a witness, it appeared the more the defense attorneys spoke, the more guilty they made their clients look.

# CHAPTER 16
## CONVICTION

I experienced only one other mistrial in my career. It was on a robbery case that I did not get to testify in. The prosecutor had the initial responding officer on the witness stand and she asked him about records checks. The officer explained the process of conducting a records check then revealed the defendant's prior arrest history. Introducing prior arrest history in that case brought a mistrial, which resulted in the defendant getting a complete pass. I couldn't blame the officer, because he was simply answering the question he was asked. Sometimes, the most difficult part of police work is watching the system work out better for the criminals than the victims.

On Wednesday, Oct. 1, 2008, I was scheduled to take the witness stand for the final time in the armed robbery trial against O.J. Simpson. The trial that had started two weeks prior, on Monday, Sept. 15, 2008, was drawing to a close. This was going to be my fourth time on the stand testifying about the investigation, and my testimony that day resulted in O.J. Simpson's defense attorneys standing up and shouting, "Mistrial!"

As I drove to the Clark County Regional Justice Center that morning, I was feeling pretty good about what I knew of the trial. Just like any other witness, I was excluded from being in the courtroom during the trial except when I was testifying and in this trial, the witnesses were also instructed to not watch the trial in any form of media. The problem with this trial was it was being aired live on multiple media formats and many of the people I had contact with on a regular basis were watching the trial. I avoided talking about it. When friends and family would start to tell me what was happening in the trial, I would politely find a way to change the direction of the conversation. I would occasionally ask people I trusted if things were going well, and they always assured me they were.

Though I had testified three other times up to this point in the trial, I had also spent most of last two weeks on standby at the courthouse. That morning, I pulled into the parking lot of the Regional Justice Center and there were fewer media trucks and vans than on the first day of the trial. As I walked to the entrance of the courthouse, I found myself walking with a handful of other officers, detectives and prosecutors who were headed to court for the hundreds of other court proceedings to be heard that day. Since the start of the trial, I received the occasional "good luck today" from those who were following the trial and this morning was no different. The encouraging words of well-wishers were almost always followed by questions: "Is it almost over?"; "Are you going to win?"; "Do you think he's going to prison?" I found that as I walked into the courthouse, those short passing conversations helped to settle my nerves for the day and even though I had testified three other times on this case, I still was a little nervous on what was my last scheduled day to testify.

My nerves had caused me to have a rough start on the first day I testified in the trial; the cameras and reporters outside the courthouse and inside the courtroom were intimidating. I had testified in many trials and hearings with suspects being accused of crimes ranging from low-level drug offenses to homicides, but nothing I had previously experienced prepared me for the pressure I felt in the trial of O.J. Simpson being accused of armed robbery. The pressure came in a variety of forms and, admittedly, most of it was self-inflicted. Selfishly, I did not want to embarrass myself. Along the same lines, the Las Vegas Metropolitan Police Department is an amazing organization and I did not want to embarrass my department. But there was also an odd heaviness that started the night I learned O.J. Simpson had committed an armed robbery in a hotel room of a Las Vegas casino. The heaviness was an enigmatic feeling that Simpson had used loopholes to beat the justice system in Los Angeles and now I felt pressure not to make a mistake that would allow that to happen again. Toward the end of my first day of testimony, my nerves had settled down and I was more comfortable.

Once I was through the security checkpoint to enter the building that morning, I was met with more well-wishers. The normal morning rush resulted in a line to get to the elevator that would have taken a few minutes to wait in. This line is often an interesting sight to watch from a distance. There are attorneys in their suits with briefcases mixed in with sex workers who have no shame in the apparel they choose to wear to court. There are victims of crimes and the suspects who committed them mixed in with witnesses and family members of everyone going to court each day. The conversations that can be overheard while waiting in the morning line for the elevator at the Regional Justice Center range from the angry bad-mouthing about how stupid the police are to professional legal strategy about upcoming court proceedings; it is a mix of cultures that can be observed in few places outside of a courthouse.

I didn't want to wait in line that morning, so I walked over to the stairs and started up. I was back to having time to focus on my testimony. Owens was calling me to the stand to clean up the loose ends that were missed by the witnesses and he also wanted me to introduce some behavior of O.J. Simpson's friends during one of Simpson's previous court hearings in this matter. When it comes to detectives testifying for the prosecution, the prosecution often leads with an open-ended question that provides the detective an opportunity to give full answers. The open-ended questions sound like, "Can you explain what happened when you responded to the Palace Station?" The defense attorneys will normally ask detectives clear-cut questions in an attempt to control the responses and they normally sound something like, "Did you respond to the Palace Station on Sept. 13, 2007?" So as I think about my testimony, I am going over in my head the things Owens had told me the night before that he wanted to cover.

As the trial started for the day, I sat alone in one of the witness rooms. About 15 minutes had passed when I heard the doors from the courtroom open. The bailiff poked his head in the room where I was sitting. "They're ready for you."

The bailiff held the door open for me as I entered the courtroom to walk to the witness stand. There was a handful of reporters and camera people in the room, and by this time in the trial, I was getting used to the sound of the cameras clicking as I walked through the middle of the gallery of seats to the witness stand. As I walked past the defense and prosecution tables, I was flooded with the odd feeling that comes every time I have testified in any jury trial: the room is quiet and every eye in the room is now watching me. As my eyes momentarily wandered around the room, I was informally greeted with head nods from the prosecution. And just like my other times testifying, O.J. Simpson also gave me a smile and a head nod. Simpson's co-defendant, Stewart, was sitting at a table next to Simpson and his attorneys. Stewart's response was more along the lines of what I had experienced in the past: his lack of eye contact and body language revealed to me he did not want to be there.

After a few questions, Owens asked me if I had an opportunity to talk with Scotto and then asked me to tell him about that exchange. It was my intent to answer as thoroughly as possible, so I began to mention his statement as well as the brief exchange after his wife, Sabrina, was escorted from the courtroom during the preliminary hearing for some inappropriate conduct toward witnesses. My response was, "Not only did I take the statement from him on the 9th, at the preliminary hearing, on one of the days and I couldn't tell you which day it was, that Mrs. Scotto was kicked out of the preliminary hearing for doing some, tampering with the witnesses—" I did not get to finish what I was saying due to the defense attorneys shouting, "Mistrial!" and "Objection! Motion for a Mistrial!" I didn't quite understand what was going on. The judge summoned all the attorneys to the bench and they spoke for a few moments. When the attorneys walked back to their tables, the judge dismissed the jury. Then, with some frustration in her voice, Judge Glass asked me to leave the courtroom.

When the judge asked me to leave the courtroom, I understood that to be a temporary removal and that I needed to stay close. After only a few minutes, I was brought back in and the jury was still out. At this point, I am still confused as to what I said to cause this problem.

When I sat back down at the witness stand without the jury present, Judge Glass said to me, "Let me make myself perfectly clear to you. I'm not and we're not going to have a discussion about what, why you said what you did, only that you said it. And that you put my case in jeopardy as far as the defense standing up and asking for a mistrial at this late stage, the very end of my case, that took us quite a lot of work to get here, as you know. And so I am going to believe that what you said was not a deliberate effort on your part to cause a problem with this case at this particular time. Over objection of the defense, I am going to admonish the jury to disregard what you said in my strongest tone in my strongest tone I possibly can to my jury. I will tell you in that whatever now Mr. Owens is going to ask you there had better not be any spontaneous answers to that are not being asked. Do you understand me detective? So if Mr. Owens asks you about Mr. Scotto being outside, we don't know, we don't care how he got there, we don't want to know why he got there, the only thing we're going to know is that you talked to him and whatever happened regarding that little bitty issue and that's it." To which all I could say was, "Yes, ma'am."

It was a painful two-minute tongue-lashing for something I honestly did not understand, but given the circumstances, I could not say anything else. In my mind, I can't stop thinking about how I said exactly what Owens had wanted me to say when we sat down to review my testimony on the night before.

What was even more confusing, I had not even got to the full point of what Owens wanted me to testify about. Not only did he want me to talk about Mrs. Scotto being kicked out of the preliminary hearing for harassing witnesses, but when she went to sit with Scotto in the atrium of the courthouse, she engaged in sexually provocative behavior that caused bailiffs to have to go and break it up. Now I was completely gun shy about saying anything Owens wanted me to say because it sucked to be lectured like that by Judge Glass and though the jury was not present, the courtroom was full and oh, yeah, it was on national television.

Before the jury was brought back in, I had to listen to Galanter argue that he should get to question me on the record about what I said and, as with Judge Glass, he keeps referencing Scotto. I was completely lost, but I was afraid to ask any questions, so I just waited. Judge Glass argued with both Galanter and Owens. I started to question myself and believe I said something about Scotto.

Judge Glass ordered the jury back into the courtroom and asked them to listen to her very carefully as she was going to give them an admonishment. She said, "Ladies and gentlemen of the jury, you are to disregard any testimony from Det. Caldwell regarding the allegation that Mr. Scotto was removed from the preliminary hearing and why he was allegedly removed from the courtroom, totally disregard, thank you." Judge Glass then instructed Owens to finish his examination of me. I was completely confused.

As Owens started questioning me, I could see one of the cameramen in the back corner of the courtroom go up to Bill Falkner, who was the head investigator of the District

Attorney's Office. Falkner took whatever message he learned from the cameraman and passed it to Roger. Roger and Owens then asked Judge Glass if they could make a representation to the court without the presence of the jury. Judge Glass was clearly not happy, but she dismissed the jury and also asked the courtroom to be emptied, including me.

I was still unclear what had happened and I did not want to talk to anyone because I felt like I had put this entire case in jeopardy. I was overwhelmed with the thought of being the reason O.J. Simpson might walk away unscathed. All of my fears of embarrassing my department and myself were rushing into my head. To top off my feeling of defeat, Deutsch, the Associated Press reporter, came and stood right next to me as she started dictating a report about the mistrial on her cell phone. I looked at her with disgust and walked away.

After about 15 minutes out in the hall, Owens came and asked me to come back in. I quickly asked if everything was all right. He responded with a smile and said, "Yes." I was not finding comfort in his answer and it was clear to me he could not take time to explain what was going on. When I followed Owens in the first set of doors into the foyer, he led me into the witness room, where Roger and Galanter were waiting for me. Owens explained how the defense heard me wrong and they believed I had said *Mr.* Scotto was ejected from the courtroom. Because he was a defense witness, had I said Mr. Scotto, it would have hurt his credibility with the jury and would not have been a true statement. Therefore, they yelled, "Mistrial!" Owens went on to explain that one of the cameramen in the courtroom was paying attention to the proceedings and was confused when he heard everyone talking about me referencing Mr. Scotto. The cameraman went back and reviewed what I said and it turns out what I said was right and the defense attorneys were wrong.

I cannot even express my emotions at that point; it was a

bittersweet moment. I didn't mess up, but I was treated like I did and was publicly scolded for something I did not do. But the case was unharmed, so I found comfort in just moving forward. With Owens and Roger sitting in the room, Galanter explained when I went back to the stand he was going to ask me a few questions to clarify what I said about Mrs. Scotto and why that was not something that was incorrect. It was an odd meeting and the defense attorneys all left together. Owens and Roger gave me a little pep talk and reassured me everything was fine. Owens said he still wanted to talk about the inappropriate behavior between Mr. and Mrs. Scotto in the atrium that had to be stopped by the bailiffs after she was kicked out of the courtroom. I wasn't sure if he was joking or not, but I apologized and said I did not feel comfortable with talking about that now. They left me in the witness room as they went back into court. I sat there with the witness room door open as the bailiff told everyone in the hallway that court was back in session.

When Judge Glass went back on the record, she said, "Thank you, I almost feel like it is a good day for having the instant replay and that is what we've just done. We're back on the record outside the presence of the jury, council and the court went and re-listened to Det. Caldwell's statement and it seems the detective was actually saying Mrs. Scotto instead of Mr. Scotto. … Since Mrs. Scotto did not testify in this trial, then all of the things that we believed had happened that caused us to all have all kinds of things happen after that, apparently did not. It is my understanding that counsel is going to handle this in the following manner. We will get the detective back on the stand. Mr. Galanter, you are going to ask some questions and in the question rather than me advising the jury that it was actually Mrs. Scotto as far as Mr., you will couch the question asking him about Mrs. Scotto?" Galanter answered, "Yes."

When I was back on the stand and the jury was called back into the courtroom, Judge Glass turned me back over to be questioned by Galanter. Galanter did not cover the question clarifying what I had said, so after a few minutes of questions, I was passed back to Owens. He asked if I was talking about Mr. or Mrs. Scotto being ejected from the courtroom and I responded by saying it was Mrs. Scotto. After I answered that question, Judge Glass turned to the jury and said, "And it reflects, now the admonition I had given you is withdrawn, just to correct the record." With the potential of having caused a mistrial being disposed of, I was dismissed as the last witness in the case.

I have spent hours thinking about and re-watching the video of that part of the trial and I have come to the simple conclusion that it was a Hail Mary pass by the defense. I believe they were looking for any reason to create some kind of drama because all their nonsensical smoke and mirrors were trumped by the simple facts of this case. Even the best defense attorney could not have changed the facts in this case; all six men involved in this armed robbery were guilty. Simpson's arrogance brushed off plea offers by the District Attorney's Office and now even his attorneys knew he was going to prison.

Both the prosecution and the defense offered their closing arguments to the jury on Oct. 2, 2008. The jury was also given its instructions for deliberation. Jury deliberation began on Oct. 3, 2008, which was 13 years to the day when O.J. Simpson was acquitted for the murders of Nicole Brown and Ron Goldman. After 13 hours of deliberation, the jury had a verdict.

I was working in an undercover capacity that day, so I was not dressed in clothes I could wear in court, but when Roger called me and told me there was a verdict, there was no way I was going to miss that. It was about 9 p.m. when Roger called me, so I started heading to the court. It was the first time I had ever been in our court building at night. The media was there in full force and there was a small crowd gathered outside the building.

There was a lottery system to get a seat in the courtroom for the reading of the verdict, but there was a seat available for me if I wanted it. I wanted to be there, but I was OK with not being in the room. I waited in the witness room that I had spent so much time in over the last two weeks. Though I could not hear everything clearly, I heard when the clerk read off the verdict of the first count of conspiracy to commit a crime as being guilty. There was a sudden increase of the clicking of cameras taking pictures as the clerk continued to read. I walked back out into the hall of the court at that point because I knew if the jury found him guilty of one charge, then they would find him guilty of all the charges. I did not wait around for the proceeding to finish. At that moment, the time and effort I put into the case over the last year all seemed worth it. I called my wife to see if she was watching and she excitedly said, "Yes!" While I was talking with her, I started to get a flood of calls to congratulate me. It was a great feeling.

Both Simpson and Stewart were taken into custody by the bailiffs immediately after the verdicts were read. Both men were taken to Clark County Detention Center, where they would await their sentencing.

# CHAPTER 17
# THE SENTENCING
# AND AFTERMATH

The flood of congratulatory phone calls I received the night Simpson was convicted was just the beginning of the personal accolades I received for my part in Simpson's conviction. It was late when the verdict was read, so it was mostly police officers and detectives who called to commend me that night. The phone calls had stopped by the time I was off at 1 a.m. and I found myself being alone with my thoughts for my drive home that night. It was a strange feeling that I could only imagine in the abstract before that night, but then it became real: I just successfully nailed the most infamous man in America and he was going to prison.

I got home and my wife was still awake; it was 2 a.m. and she wanted to tell me about the calls she had with her friends and family and how excited people were. The next morning, I was woken up by a phone call. It was Bob Whiteley, a longtime friend and, at the time of the conviction, we were working on the same squad. Bob wanted to make sure my head hadn't gotten too big to come into work and that I knew he wasn't going to let me slack off just because I caught O.J. Simpson. After a few laughs, we got off the phone so I could start getting ready to go into work. Before I was able to get ready, my mom called. Being from Southern California, my mom and dad had hung on every twist and turn of the Simpson murder trial. My mom called to tell me how and all her friends in her retirement community had watched every minute of the trial in Las Vegas and she had to tell me how thrilled everyone was. My dad passed away in 2006 and she wanted to also tell me how proud my dad would have been.

The day after the conviction, I was still working an undercover assignment with a multijurisdictional task force.

I was used in a very limited undercover capacity because of my recent media coverage. I was working with officers from other cities in Nevada, Arizona and California and agents from the ATF. I walked into the same office building I had walked into the past few days with the same detectives and agents, but today was different. When I walked in, there were already about 20 guys in the room—20 cops with beards and long hair, and most were covered with tattoos. They were the same guys who I briefed with the day before, only today when I walked in the room, every one of them started clapping.

Over the next couple weeks at work, I was treated like a superstar. Cops I didn't know came up to me to congratulate me and emailed me with thoughtful comments about the investigation and conviction. A couple of FBI agents from the Los Angeles Field Office stopped by our task force office to meet me and share stories of when they were rookie agents in Los Angeles during the murder trial.

It wasn't just cops, though. For a few weeks after the conviction, I had neighbors stop by when they saw my car coming home just to tell me, "Thank you." A few times when I was out shopping with my family in Las Vegas, I heard older couples debating if I was the detective from the O.J. Simpson trial. One of my favorite moments happened in a Kmart about a week after the sentencing. An older gentleman who looked like he was in his 60s or 70s approached me. He walked up to me and extended his right hand out to shake my hand. Before I could meet his hand with mine, he was already smiling and said, "Thank you for what you did." And without any further conversation, he just walked away.

After a month or so passed, those moments started to get fewer and farther between. I found myself vacillating on how much I liked being associated with convicting O.J. Simpson. Most of the time, I enjoyed the association and the favor that came along with it. I enjoyed my captain introducing me to the Nevada attorney general as the guy who put O.J. away. I enjoyed the connections through the District Attorney's Office because most of the prosecutors followed the Simpson trial. I occasionally became frustrated when I felt like someone represented the O.J. Simpson case as the embodiment of my work, rather than part of the body of my work. I had worked far more complex cases and had already had a good reputation as a detective before O.J. Simpson, so I did not want to be represented as a one-hit wonder who only put O.J. Simpson in prison.

After the trial, I received a few requests for media interviews through my department's Public Information Office and was approached by one author who offered to write a book for me. Though on one level I enjoyed the attention, there was another part of me that just wanted to go back to my normal work so I could shift my primary focus back to my faith and my family.

I knew my connection with putting O.J. Simpson in prison had paved the way for most any assignment I wanted to pursue on the department. But at that point in my life, my career goals had drastically shifted away from climbing the career ladder; I wanted to serve my church more and make sure I did not miss any more time away from my kids than I had to. An opportunity presented itself for me to become a resident officer for my department in the town I lived in, about 60 miles northeast of Las Vegas. It was a substantial pay raise, but viewed by most as taking a step backwards in my career. However, it was best for my family. When I took the position as a resident officer, I went back to wearing a uniform and being a first responder. I loved being able to serve my community in that capacity.

On Dec. 5, 2008, O.J. Simpson and Clarence Stewart were sentenced by Judge Jackie Glass to serve a sentence of 15 to 33 years in a Nevada state prison with eligibility for parole after nine years.

As Judge Glass sentenced Simpson, she explained how the evidence was overwhelming in this case. She addressed the issues of how violent the encounter was and how great the potential for harm to a tourist was when he and his armed men brought a gun to that violent encounter in a small hotel room at a packed hotel and casino in Las Vegas. As she explained the sentence she was issuing, she noted she was not there to punish him for what has happened to him previously in the justice system, that she was sentencing him based on this case. Judge Glass broke down each individual count and sentenced both Simpson and Stewart within the stated ranges of penalties for each one of the crimes they were convicted of.

I'm not a judge and I have never experienced having to sentence someone to prison. But speaking as a robbery detective, I have never seen someone get that harsh of a sentence for a first-time robbery. I do believe O.J. Simpson is the perfect example of why there is a range of punishments available to a judge to sentence individuals found guilty of crime. It is my opinion that the totality of O.J.'s circumstances merited his punishment and he deserved every moment he spent in prison. I had a great sense of accomplishment in my work and I do feel like justice was served.

Over the years, I did not closely follow what was happening with Simpson in prison. On two occasions, I called a friend in the Inspector General's Office to find out if tabloid stories were true and quickly found out they were completely false. I did not pry for details, I was just looking to see if he really did get beat up over cookies or if he was on death's doorstep. In fact, I was surprised to learn he wasn't causing major problems at all.

It wasn't just tabloid media who got facts wrong in dealing with O.J. Simpson's armed robbery case. Years after he was sentenced to prison, I could mention to people that I was the detective on the O.J. Simpson case and nine times out of 10, they respond by asking me if I was talking about the time O.J. took his own property back. That was a better story than the truth; it's what the media reported happened and is still what I find many people believe. I was disappointed the first time I heard the media report that Simpson had simply taken his own property back. The lack of a desire for truth was frustrating. I have found truth in our culture is no longer objective and measurable, to the detriment of our society, truth has become relative to the individual. I am probably hypersensitive to this because of my experience with the O.J. Simpson case and watching the media focus on what drives emotions rather than focusing on the truth.

In 2015, there was a show called "Making a Murderer" that was getting national media attention and some of the officers I worked with were even watching it. I heard people talking about how the detectives appeared to manipulate interviews and coerce statements. I found myself interested enough to watch. I don't know all the details of the case and I would not want to form an opinion based on a TV show, but when I watched the interviews, I saw good police work. If I didn't allow the tone of the show to manipulate me, I saw good police work. I found myself upset when I heard people talking about the detectives in this show because I know how easy it is for half-truths to be represented as fact and how controversy makes a good story.

My experience with O.J. Simpson and the media taught me that truth is relative and if the media can make a story more controversial than it is, many of them will regardless of what is true. I have become skeptical of most news reporting on anything high profile. If Tom Brady's footballs were accidently low on pressure, there is no story, but creating a conspiracy makes news that goes on and on. If Officer Darren Wilson was defending himself from being beaten by Michael Brown, then there is no story, but if a police officer shot an innocent kid, then a story is created that creates more stories. Truth is too often sacrificed at the altar of anarchy. Rules no longer govern. It is all about pandering to the emotions of the day to sell a story.

As an experienced investigator, I recognize the need to

seek truth even when it is hard to find. I hope my integrity causes me to seek out truth even when I cannot obtain facts firsthand. After the trial was over, I wanted to know more about the law enforcement view of the Ron Goldman and Nicole Brown murders. I read Mark Fuhrman's "Murder in Brentwood" and Marcia Clark's "Without a Doubt." I tried to objectively take two different perspectives from the same side of a coin and see how I would feel if I had been involved in the murder trials. I cannot fairly say who murdered Nicole Brown and Ron Goldman, but from an outside perspective, there does appear to have been an overwhelming amount of evidence pointing to O.J. Simpson. But because I do have respect for our criminal justice system, even when I disagree, I honor its verdict and I trust ultimate justice belongs to the Lord.

Since Simpson's conviction in 2008, I had mostly let the case be part of my past. I would use my involvement in the case as an icebreaker from time to time. I have always enjoyed O.J. Simpson jokes and comments among friends, but I never sought out opportunities to publicly share about the investigation. Suddenly in 2016, FX came out with "The People v. O.J. Simpson: American Crime Story" and people start asking me about O.J. Simpson again. I had friends and family telling me they would write a book if they were me. My wife and I talked about it and prayed about it. It seemed like a good time to try and memorialize my experience. I had gone back to school and obtained a master of arts in theological studies and was approaching retiring from the LVMPD in early 2017. My wife and I then planned to pursue serving Christ in full-time pastoral ministry. As I started writing, all of the memories and experiences came rushing back into my life. Because I was so close to the case, I missed how others outside of the investigation might have an interest in reading about the investigation and what actually happened. I missed how people might have a genuine interest in their own idea of justice being served. I missed how many people had invested their emotions in the murders of Nicole Brown and Ron Goldman. I may have misread the interest over the years, but as I sat down and started writing, I realized my reluctance to write about my experience was largely an issue of pride. I did not want to be successful in putting America's most infamous figure in prison and then fail at writing about how it happened.

It is my deepest hope that this book provides those who over the years have personally invested their emotions in the personality of O.J. Simpson can walk away with a better understanding of what happened in Las Vegas that landed him in a Nevada State Prison.

*For More News About Andy Caldwell and
Room 1203, Signup For Our Newsletter:*

**http://wbp.bz/newsletter**

*Word-of-mouth is critical to an author's long-
term success. If you appreciated
this book please leave a review on the Amazon sales page:*

**http://wbp.bz/Rm1203a**

## Another Great True Crime
## Read From WildBlue Press

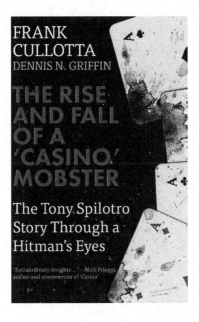

In The Rise and Fall of Tony Spilotro, Frank tells the true story of Tony Spilotro, his rise up the ladder to become an Outfit boss, his subsequent fall from power and murder at the hands of the Outfit. Frank also talks about the many murders Tony committed, ordered or planned. In several instances Frank names the killers in cases that are officially unsolved. It's a story that only Frank Cullotta could tell.

Read More: **http://wbp.bz/mobster**

## Another Great True Crime
## Read From WildBlue Press

"Best True Crime Book of 2015" (Suspense Magazine) A "Sin City" cop recounts his efforts to catch one of the most prolific criminals to ever walk the neon-lit streets of Las Vegas. "If you like mayhem, madness, and suspense, Repeat Offender is the book to read."(Aphrodite Jones, New York Times bestselling author)

Read More: **http://wbp.bz/ro**

See even more at:
**http://wbp.bz/tc**

# More True Crime You'll Love From WildBlue Press

### RAW DEAL by Gil Valle

RAW DEAL: The Untold Story of the NYPD's "Cannibal Cop" is the memoir of Gil Valle, written with co-author Brian Whitney. It is part the controversial saga of a man who was imprisoned for "thought crimes," and a look into an online world of dark sexuality and violence that most people don't know exists, except maybe in their nightmares.

**wbp.bz/rawdeal**

### BETRAYAL IN BLUE by Burl Barer & Frank C. Girardot Jr.

Adapted from Ken Eurell's shocking personal memoir, plus hundreds of hours of exclusive interviews with the major players, including former international drug lord, Adam Diaz, and Dori Eurell, revealing the truth behind what you won't see in the hit documentary THE SEVEN FIVE.

**wbp.bz/bib**

### THE POLITICS OF MURDER by Margo Nash

*"A chilling story about corruption, political power and a stacked judicial system in Massachusetts."*–John Ferak, bestselling author of FAILURE OF JUSTICE.

**wbp.bz/pom**

### FAILURE OF JUSTICE by John Ferak

If the dubious efforts of law enforcement that led to the case behind MAKING A MURDERER made you cringe, your skin will crawl at the injustice portrayed in FAILURE OF JUSTICE: A Brutal Murder, An Obsessed Cop, Six Wrongful Convictions. Award-winning journalist and bestselling author John Ferak pursued the story of the Beatrice 6 who were wrongfully accused of the brutal, ritualistic rape and murder of an elderly widow in Beatrice, Nebraska, and then railroaded by law enforcement into prison for a crime they did not commit.

**wbp.bz/foj**

CPSIA information can be obtained
at www.ICGtesting.com
Printed in the USA
FSOW04n0813230717
36767FS